PRACTICAL MINISTRY

IN THE REAL WORLD

PRACTICAL MINISTRY

IN THE REAL WORLD

ROBERT C. SHANNON
J. MICHAEL SHANNON

COLLEGE PRESS PUBLISHING COMPANY • JOPLIN, MISSOURI

Cover Design by
Daryl Williams

Library of Congress Cataloging-in-Publication Data

Shannon, Robert, 1930–
    Practical ministry in the real world / Robert C. Shannon,
J. Michael Shannon.
        p.   cm.
    Includes bibliographical references.
    ISBN 0-89900-785-6 (pbk.)
    1. Pastoral theology.   2. Clergy—Office.   3. Pastoral
theology—Christian Churches and Churches of Christ.
4. Christian Churches and Churches of Christ—Clergy.
I. Shannon, J. Michael   II. Title.
BV660.2.S48 1997
253—dc21   97-24824
                                                          CIP

To our students past, present
and future. Never give up!

TABLE OF CONTENTS

INTRODUCTION

The faculty of a leading institution of higher learning was in the midst of a long discussion of course offerings. The topic was academic courses versus practical courses. Finally one of the professors had had enough. He reminded the faculty that the antonym to *practical* was not *academic*. It is possible to so emphasize "academic" courses that the whole education process becomes impractical insofar as ministry is concerned. On the other hand, it is possible to so emphasize practical courses that there is no solid foundation of conceptual knowledge on which to build a ministry. It is essential that ministry have a deep cognitive base. It is equally essential that one know how to communicate knowledge and how to develop the life of a congregation in a practical way. Everything one learns is of value, but if you cannot lead a soul to Christ, comfort the sorrowing, guide the confused and lead people to their full potential of service, then that knowledge is ineffective. This book is unabashedly practical. It attempts to cover everything the minister of a local church does from the time he puts his shoes on in the morning until he takes them off at night.

The book is directed to the preaching minister. Other staff members will also find it useful. Associate ministers will find much here that will be germane to their work. We have tried to write the book in a personal style, and so we have used the second person as if we were sitting across the desk from a preacher and discussing what we have learned, experienced and observed.

Since everybody's life experience is different, there will be much that is of necessity subjective — but we have tried to be as objective as possible. However, we must write from what has proven to be true, effective and workable in our own ministries. Our collective experience includes churches large and small, rural and urban, new and established, growing, static and declining. If our advice seems wrong, then check your own experience and observation, as well as the experience of others in the ministry before you decide on a different path.

We have tried to bring two different generational viewpoints to the book — hence there are two authors. Each generation has something unique to contribute to our understanding of how ministry is done. While we do not see everything from the same vantage point, we found ourselves in agreement at most points — and only rarely in disagreement.

Changing times will mean changing the ways we work. We have tried to be conscious of that in each chapter, and especially in the final chapter. We have written so that you, like Timothy, may fulfill your ministry.

CHAPTER ONE

THE MINISTER'S PERSONAL LIFE

Personal Integrity

Paul told the preacher, Timothy, to be an example (1 Tim. 4:12). He who preaches kindness must be kind. He who preaches about prayer must pray. He who preaches about purity must keep his own life pure. One cannot preach about truthfulness and then not *be* truthful. One cannot preach about honesty and then cheat. One cannot speak against deceitfulness and then deceive.

The preacher's family should also be an example to the congregation. His wife and children should be models for the church to follow.

This is not to say that the preacher is perfect, nor is it to say that his family is perfect. A preacher should not expect his children to be any better than all Christians should be. It is a mistake for a preacher to say to his children, "You cannot do that because your father is a preacher." That's a certain way to ensure that they will grow up resenting the church. One should only say that a thing should not be done because it is wrong.

A minister's wife should not be expected to be an unpaid assistant minister. She should certainly support her husband and his work, but her first obligation is to

11

be a wife and mother. Her obligations to the church come after that. She should be willing to do as much as any other wife in the congregation. She should not be expected to do more.

The minister should spend time with his family. He should not be a stranger to his wife and children. On the other hand, he should not use family concerns as an excuse to avoid work that needs to be done for the church. It is always difficult to balance these two demands. Church work will necessarily keep him out of the home much of the time. But one night each week should be set aside for family. The church should not cause us to neglect our families, and our families should not cause us to neglect the church.

The minister symbolizes far more than himself. Paul describes us as ambassadors (2 Cor. 5:20). We represent the church. When we walk down the street, people not only see us, they see our church. Beyond that, in some sense we also represent Jesus Christ — and God! We must be conscious of what this demands. We know that we are a poor representation of deity. We know that we are only human. But we do not need to continually remind our congregations that we are human. Nor do we need to keep confessing our own sinfulness. They will know enough of our faults as it is.

As ministers we have inherited an enormous reservoir of trust. People trust us with their money, with their children, with their wives, and with their darkest secrets. This reservoir of trust was laid down by generations of preachers who have gone before us. We must never take that trust lightly. We must do nothing that will diminish that trust. We must do all that we can to add to that trust.

Someone took a survey of what people in a congregation expect from their preacher. Number one was "service without regard to acclaim." Number two was "personal integrity." Number three was "an example." Every minister can do these things well. We do not all have the same degree of talent. Some preachers are more gifted than others. Some can preach better than others. Some are better evangelists than others. Some are better pastors than others. But all can excel equally in these three things, and should.

People respect preachers. We get that without earning it. But when we earn what we have already received we lay down a deposit for those who will come after us. On the other hand, we must not allow people to deify us — to make us gods. For then we may be tempted to substitute our sovereignty for His.

We must not use people to advance our chosen goals. We must not use people to build up our own vanity and sense of self-worth. Put simply, we must not use people. We must help people to be used by God.

We must continually examine and re-examine our own motives. We must know that our motives are pure. We must keep our integrity. Integrity means that we are what we appear to be. It means we have nothing to hide. It means we always pay our bills. It means that we always tell the truth. It does not mean that we must tell all the truth we know. There is a difference between frankness and honesty. We must be honest. We do not have to be frank. Kindness demands that we not answer all questions put to us; that we not comment on all things that come up in the conversation. We do not have to tell all the truth we know, but we do have to tell nothing but the truth.

Integrity demands that every day we do an honest day's work. Integrity means that we are dependable. It means that we are transparent. We need not reveal our secret struggles with temptation or doubt. That is our private affair. But we must live so there is never a need to hide anything; so that there are no subjects to be avoided and no eyes to be avoided.

Our work schedule must include time for study and reflection and prayer. It must also include time in the community and time with our members. If we come to our members only in times of crisis, then we come as a stranger and we're not going to be able to help. But if we are known as a friend, we can minister the grace of God in crisis times. One man said, "A home-going preacher makes a church-going people." It's true. Visitation in homes and in the community informs our preaching so that we preach about real issues and real questions rather than vague abstractions. It is so tempting to preach about what interests us instead of what blesses them.

The most valuable thing we have to spend is time. We must spend it properly and spend it well. The management of our time is the most difficult challenge we face. For we must find time to know our people. We must find time to know the Bible. And we must find time to know God — personally. The best use of our time is the greatest challenge we face.

There is also the temptation to preach what people want to hear or what we want to say rather than what people need to hear and what God wants said. To preach what the people want is to simply verbalize the opinions they already hold rather than to instruct and enlarge. To preach what I want to say is only to use the pulpit to vent my own anger, frustration or anxiety. To preach what people need is to preach what God wants said, and that is our goal.

Devotional Life

How do you keep your own devotional life fresh and meaningful? Set aside the first few minutes of the work day for personal devotions. You can combine this with planning and goal-setting for the day to make for an invaluable start to your day's work. You may also have devotions with the staff, but that is a different matter. Go to the sanctuary alone. Sit where the people sit. Read some verses from the Bible. Read some sermons from the masters. Read your Scriptures in an alternate

14

translation and familiar passages will come to you with new meaning. Try not to see them just as homiletics texts, but as food for the soul. Choose a hymn or chorus and sing it aloud or to yourself. You could try reading from a book of prayers, including the *Book of Common Prayer* of the Episcopal Church. Those carefully written prayers will help keep your own prayers alive and fresh. Then pray your own prayer for yourself and your people. Some ministers select each day, in alphabetical order six members of their congregation and pray for them until they have prayed for every family and member. Pray for those who have special needs. Pray for your family and yourself. The apostles in Jerusalem thought the ministry of the word and prayer were the two most important activities of their ministries. They let nothing get in the way of them. Let nothing short of a real emergency keep you from this devotional time. Begin each day with it and it will bless you beyond description. It's not that we would be superstitious about this. If you miss this time, it doesn't doom your day. But if you consistently have this time, you will feel a greater power in your life and ministry and it will bless you beyond understanding. There is the ever present danger for us who hold holy things. It is that the holy things become commonplace and cease to be holy to us.

Morality

No ministerial problem has received as much attention as the incidence of sexual indiscretion. No one knows if it is more prevalent than in the past. We may assume that since it is more prevalent generally in the population, it is probably more prevalent in the ministry today. It is certainly more apparent. These matters used to be handled with confidentiality. Now, the baby-boomer tendency towards transparency makes every pastoral indiscretion an event.

15

It is certainly damaging to the cause. No one denies that. Can it be defeated? Most likely, but only if every minister understands he is perfectly capable of committing adultery. If he knows he is capable of it, then he can take pains to avoid it.

What are the causes of sexual indiscretion?

They are as varied as the people who commit the sin.

Of course the problem is sin itself. We will make no attempt to disguise that. There are reasons, however, that ministers who genuinely love the Lord get caught up in this sin.

Often it is a poor self-image. Someone makes the minister feel more wanted, desired or respected.

Sometimes it is depression. Depressed people will look for passion wherever they can find it. Sexual passion is a strong emotion and gives temporary relief from the banality of the depressed state.

Some give in to relieve boredom. Kierkegaard believed that boredom was the root of most sins.

Sometimes ministers are prone to this problem because of the professional intimacy fostered by the counseling a minister does.

Obviously, marital problems can exacerbate the problem, but these are not the central issues, but often only an excuse. Some spouses who cheat report that the marriage relationship was fine. In some cases the person was looking for excitement, not a new spouse.

How does this affect the preacher in particular, apart from the dynamics of sexual indiscretion in general?

Some amount of sexual attraction is normal. It is difficult to describe when normal attraction turns to lust, but most can tell you when it has happened.

Often these situations begin innocently enough and the parties involved try to tell themselves it is merely friendship. Even a close friendship with a member of the opposite sex can place enormous strain on a marriage.

16

Sometimes these problems begin in the process of counseling. Intimate details are discussed. Sometimes the counselor develops a real empathy for the counselee that later becomes confused. A counselee will tell things to a minister that he or she would never speak of anywhere else.

However the situation begins, it is then fed by fantasy and lust. It is amazing what a person obsessed by fantasy and lust will do. They risk everything — job, marriage and reputation.

How do ministers defend against sexual indiscretion?

First, *accept the challenge of making your marriage the best it can be.* The test of true romance is not the ability to get a stranger interested in you, but the ability to keep the one who knows all your faults interested in you.

Always consider the consequences. A minister who is tempted might well ask, "Am I willing to pay the enormous price this act will require? Am I willing to lose my church, wife, children, friends, reputation and integrity?" A good dose of reality can sometimes serve as a splash of cold water.

Maintain a thoroughly professional approach in your personal counseling. Keep the meetings to one hour. Hold the sessions at the church office. It might be a good idea to develop a network of trusted older women who could counsel the females.

Do not put yourself in a position to be alone with a woman. This includes restaurants, church retreats, and even in the automobile.

Have a friend who can hold you accountable. This may not be possible for everyone, but it will be possible for most. Every minister needs a confidant. It is not wise to make that person a member of your church. Another trusted minister friend is probably the best choice.

The issue is not forgiveness. Of course a Christian can be forgiven of adultery. The issue is leadership. A

17

person can be clean before God, but still have inflicted much damage to the cause of Christ.

Feelings of Unworthiness

While ministers set a higher standard, they dare not set an impossible one. This places too great a burden on a mere mortal. Preaching the gospel of Jesus Christ is a rare privilege and heavy responsibility. Is anyone worthy of such a responsibility? The simple answer is, "No, of course not." We aren't worthy of receiving the gospel, much less ministering it. That sense of unworthiness should not deter us from our mission, though. That unworthiness is part of the human condition; we can do nothing about it. Every person on this earth shares this problem. If people deferred from preaching the gospel until they were worthy, no one would preach it. It is important to note that God has always used imperfect people, mainly because that's all he has to work with. In addition, God loves to manifest his power through imperfect people. His strength is displayed in our weakness. I want to be careful not to oversell my case. Yes, we should try to be the best we can be, but we minister while we are engaged in this lifelong pursuit. Many ministers struggle with the diffidence caused by the gap between their beliefs and their performance. Some ministers never put this difficulty to rest or find the perspective that allows them to be fully functional. Maybe it would be helpful if we looked at a sketch of some of the people God has used in the past. After bringing forth these witnesses and listening to their stories, it will be difficult for us to try to maintain a belief that God can't use us. All of the men we will look at are noteworthy. All of them made a significant impact. All of them had a significant flaw. We don't look at these lives to give ourselves an excuse for immoral behavior. We look for one reason. We want to recognize that God works with flawed clay.

18

Can God use a man who once had problems with drink? Just ask Noah. Noah was the only decent man of his day. God saw fit to save only Noah and his family from the cleansing flood. Yet, Noah was not without flaw. The Bible records that after Noah and his family settled in the new world, Noah had trouble with the consumption of wine. Why should I mince words? He got staggering drunk. It led to an embarrassing and unsavory family problem. Noah proves the point that great men have great faults, but God uses them.

Can God use a person who once had trouble bending the truth? Just ask Abraham. Remember how Abraham on two occasions used a lie to avoid facing a difficult situation? He cooked up a little lie about his wife. Abraham ended up looking less virtuous than the pagan rulers he was dealing with. Even in spite of this, he is lifted up as an example of faith for the world to emulate. The Bible does not endorse his dishonesty, but it does acknowledge it.

Can God use a man who once was a schemer? Just ask Jacob. Jacob schemed his way to the top. He outwitted his brother, father and father-in-law. Practically everything Jacob had, he had gotten by his own ingenuity. Yet one night Jacob learned that some blessings cannot be received by scheming. He wrestled with the angel of the Lord and stubbornly held on for a blessing. In this act, Jacob was admitting that he was powerless to devise a way to receive the kind of blessing he wanted most. Some blessings only come from the hand of God. They must be received by faith. Even though Jacob was imperfect, God called him Israel, and his name is remembered even today in the name of the nation of his heritage.

Can God use a man who once was a braggart? Just ask Joseph. I know that Joseph was a righteous man. He was not, however, a perfect man. There is more than normal bragging in his talk of dreams and people bowing down to him. He may have even worn his specially adorned coat with a certain swagger that says, "Hey, look at me." He enjoyed his favored position and lorded it over his brothers. That doesn't mean he deserved what happened to him. Being threatened with his life, sold into slavery, being falsely accused and placed in jail went way beyond the offenses he committed against his brothers. But God used his trials to sand down his pride and to provide a blessing for his people. Once again we see how God uses imperfect people.

Can God use a man who had a quick temper? Just ask Moses. In a fit of righteous anger, Moses let his wrath go unchecked and killed an Egyptian and buried him in the sand. He spent forty years in anonymity, thinking about his behavior. Had God not confronted him with the dramatic burning bush, Moses might have spent the rest of his life in the wilderness. Even after returning to leadership Moses threw down the Ten Commandments and broke them. Not only did God use Moses, but he used him in an incredible and mighty way. Later he would be called Moses the Meek. What a designation for a man with such a quick temper!

Can God use a person who battled with fear? Just ask Gideon. When we first meet Gideon, he is threshing grain in a winepress for fear. Not a very likely candidate for leadership, but God made the best of him. He led Gideon and his pitifully small army on to a great victory. This man, who once was huddled in a winepress, faced the enemy with an army of three hundred, equipped with trumpets, torches and pitchers. How can a fearful man lead such a small, poorly equipped army? God used him in spite of his timidity. Gideon learned that no army is poorly equipped when God is on their side.

Can God use a man who once had an eye for the ladies? Just ask David. Here is a man who sinned the sin that ministers are being caught in with ever increasing regularity. Still, he was a man after God's own heart. When he was confronted with his sin, he wasted no time. He repented. Certainly a man's behavior in this area is a crucial measure of spiritual maturity. My point is not to say that we should take sexual sin lightly. When Nathan confronted David, he shared with him a serious reason to avoid sexual sin. He told David that his sin had given the enemies of God reason to blaspheme. That should be a strong deterrent. No, we are in no way diminishing the importance of fidelity. We are only saying that even this very serious sin is not beyond God's powerful grace.

Can God use a person who has battled depression? Just ask Elijah. Elijah had just experienced his greatest victory with the contests over the prophets of Baal, when he heard a price had been put on his head. He fled to the wilderness where he sat under a tree and beseeched God to take his life. Nevertheless, God reinvigorated him and sent him on to win more victories. Elijah heard the still, small voice, the sound of silence and felt God's strengthening power. Elijah has become for us the model of the courageous prophet.

Can God use a person who had a troubled home life? Just ask Hosea. Very few preachers could survive the problems Hosea had to go through. There was trouble in the parsonage for sure. Gomer, Hosea's wife, had been unfaithful. Hosea not only forgave her, but bought her back out of slavery. He took her back into the home. God used Hosea's love for his wife to be a picture of God's love for his people. God can use Hosea to encourage us as well.

Can God use a person with a big mouth? Just ask Peter. Peter's lack of self-control is legendary. He not only said the wrong things, he sometimes said them with oaths. God used that tongue to preach the first gospel sermon, on the day of Pentecost. A man who once was afraid to admit to a little girl that he even knew Jesus, was not afraid to stand before thousands and proclaim the gospel. God let him write a portion of holy Scripture. Later he even gave up his very life. If God can use Peter, don't you think he can use you?

Can God use a person who struggled with ambition? Just ask John. John and his brother wanted to sit at the right and left hand of Jesus. John's brother became the first of the twelve to surrender his life for the gospel. John lived a long life and learned to surrender his ambitions. He became the apostle of love. In his own Gospel, he doesn't even mention himself by name. In his Apocalypse, he talks of throwing down our crowns before the Lord God. If God can use John, he can use you.

Can God use a man who has struggled with selfish pride? Just ask Paul. I don't think it is taking too many liberties to say that Paul had trouble with pride. He says of himself, "I was a Pharisee of the Pharisees." You don't have to read too carefully between the lines to see that Paul constantly struggled with this problem. Yet no man ever gave as much of himself to Christ as Paul. He lost health, wealth and life itself for Christ. He became so humbled, that God allowed him to write more of the New Testament than any other person.

This was a quick visit with a number of witnesses. We could have examined countless others. There is only one purpose in all of this — to make one point. God can use anyone. It is evidence of God's sovereignty that he can accomplish his purposes with greatly flawed vessels. It is not my desire to release you from the obligation to get control of your life. Remember in Greek legend, Achilles was dipped in the river Styx to protect his body from injury. The only part of him that was vulnerable was the place on his heel, where his mother's hand held him as he was dipped in the river. In battle Achilles was killed when an arrow pierced the only spot where he was vulnerable. It is in our best interest to protect ourselves. Our faithfulness also honors God. I cannot exempt you from being under God's authority. But don't let your failures interfere with your calling. The Bible is honest about the faults of its heroes, but we must remember that the faults in these men's lives were the exception, not the rule. We must also remember that with God's help they triumphed over their faults and their failures. If they can, so can you. Wouldn't it be a form of arrogance to say that God cannot use you? That would be saying that you can make a mess God can't clean up. That would make you more powerful than God. Even while God is working on you, he will use you. God doesn't need our help, but he has chosen to make us partners in his work. You are not worthy, but you are wanted.

CHAPTER TWO

THE MINISTER AND PREACHING

In an age of specialization, something needs to be said for preaching. There are many excellent and essential ministries in the church, but nothing will ever surpass preaching. Even in specialized ministries such as youth ministry, Christian education, etc., any minister would be more effective if he learned how to communicate the word of God with power. It is beyond the scope of this chapter to give detailed instruction, but no survey of ministry is complete without some attention to effective preaching. If you are in the senior ministry, the congregation will forgive other deficiencies, if you don't bore them on Sunday morning.

Few, if any preachers, aspire to mediocrity. No one ever says, "I would really like to be an average preacher." Still, there are many average preachers. Not all of us can hope to enter the preaching hall of fame, but we can be better and we can preach in such a way as to be pleasing to God and helpful to people. Let's look together at the essential skills and attitudes necessary to make a preacher great. We will look at these skills under two headings: the preacher in his study and the preacher in his pulpit.

In the Study

Any preacher who wants to excel will have to invest the time. Many of the great preachers report spending as much as twenty hours for every sermon. That is not likely to be practical for most of us. Nevertheless, the preacher will notice that as he spends more time, he will produce better sermons. A sermon is like barbecue — it is best when slow-cooked. It is not possible to develop a mature thought without giving hours to sermon preparation.

A preacher who wants to excel must study the masters. This does not mean slavishly copying them. But all great performers, whether in drama, music, art or sports, study those who have already mastered the process.

A preacher who wants to excel must become a scholar. This is not to suggest that every preacher needs to be able to readily translate the New Testament. There is always a place for specialists in academic subjects. Even a physician appeals to specialists. As preachers we are general practitioners, but we must know how to read and understand the experts. A preacher can only rely on charm and winsome delivery for a short time. Eventually we must study. This is hard work. That is why it is often avoided.

D.W. Cleverly Ford once said that the insoluble dilemma of the preacher was that without a congregation he had no one to preach to and with a congregation he had no time to prepare to preach. Notice that he called it "an insoluble dilemma." We can, however, manage the problem if we make careful use of time. That means making double use of time. You will spend many hours in your car, driving to hospitals, homes, meetings. You can use this time to think creatively about your sermon for next Sunday. Of course, it is hard to prepare without your tools, but it is possible. You can make a note of this or that you wish to research when you get back to your study. You will know exactly what you are seeking. You will not be

26

spinning your wheels. You spend time waiting in the dentist's office, the doctor's office, or for a counselee who is late for his appointment. You can use these bits of time creatively.

It is not the case that you must have a block of several uninterrupted hours to be creative. You can turn the creative process on and you can turn it off. Using these lost bits of time will greatly enlarge the time available for sermon preparation. When you do this, a subtle thing happens. Your sermon lies in the subconscious part of your mind. It will come to the front as you converse with someone or as you go about other tasks. This multiplies your preparation time. Most busy ministers will find that six or seven hours a week is the most they can muster for focused, intensive sermon preparation. But you can double or triple that time by using this plan.

A preacher who wants to excel must be creative. Not all of us will be equally creative. But a sermon is more than an exegetical lecture.

A sermon should be interesting. Someone has said that we dare not make the living Word sound like a dead letter. We don't need to make the Bible interesting. It already is. We need to make our sermons interesting.

Dorothy Sayers said that you may call the Bible exhilarating or you may call it devastating, that you may call it revelation or call it rubbish, but that if you call it dull, then words have no meaning. "If this is dull," she wrote, "then what in Heaven's name deserves to be called interesting?"

A sermon should be relevant to life. Once again, it's not necessary to make the Bible relevant. It already is relevant. We only need to show that relevance.

A sermon should be a thing of beauty. It does not denigrate a diamond when you put it in a setting of gold. It honors the diamond. It does not denigrate Scripture to put it in a beautiful setting. It honors the text. It honors the occasion. It honors the listener. We must be careful here. If we overdo it, then attention is drawn from the truth to the medium by which the truth is conveyed. Then it is like an overdressed person. The attention is diverted from the person to the clothing. We don't want that to happen. On the other hand, we do a disservice to truth if we make no effort to present it attractively.

So we look for new ways to tell old truths. We look for new words for old ideas. We look for new illustrations, new similes, new metaphors. We develop our vocabularies. As long as we avoid technical jargon, there is little danger that people will not understand. The passive vocabulary is always greater than the active. They may not use beautiful words but they will understand them.

What qualities should a minister strive for?

A minister should strive for fidelity. Is the sermon faithful to the teaching of Scripture?

A minister should strive for clarity. Did the congregation know what he was talking about?

A minister should strive for variety. Does he preach the same kind of sermon over and over again?

A minister should strive for practicality. Can his sermon be applied to modern people with modern problems and modern modes of expression? When Pinson and Fant completed their massive multivolume set *A Treasury of Great Preaching,* formerly entitled *Twenty Centuries of Great Preaching,* they strove to determine what was the common factor among all the preachers they had studied. The book contained so many eras, theological persuasions and styles. The word they came up with was "relevant." People consider great preaching relevant to their existence.

A minister should strive for creativity. Has the old story been communicated in a fresh way? A good sermon is not just an exegetical lecture.

The preaching ministry presents a great challenge. It is a challenge to creative skills. First, there is the sheer volume of it. The cost in terms of time alone is tremendous. A minister who preaches two sermons a week produces between 300,000 and 400,000 words a year. That is more than a full-time author. It equals seven full-length novels each year. In addition to that, he makes his calls, directs his program, and serves as counselor for the distressed, financial expert for the Board, and referee for the intrachurch quarrels.

Beyond that, a further challenge lies. Unlike any other of the fine arts, the minister must be creative and original within strict bounds. First is the boundary of time. He must do what he does in twenty-five minutes. Second, he must limit himself to proper language clearly understood by the common man. He is limited in subject matter to Christian doctrine, limited in viewpoint by the Bible. Yet within these severe limitations, he must produce something that is both old and new, both orthodox and fresh; and he must do it fifty-two Sundays a year. No writer, no artist, no sculptor, no composer has ever faced such a task. What a challenge!

The minister has many responsibilities. That in itself is a real challenge. To be scholar, evangelist, pastor, preacher, teacher, counselor, fund-raiser, publicist, journalist, troubleshooter, office manager, promoter, and friend of dogs and children represent a wide range of abilities and skills. No man does them all well, but it is a thrill to serve in a profession that demands such variety. What a challenge!

The preaching ministry, however, *is* the most rewarding of all disciplines. The author cannot see the response of his readers, nor the artist the response of his viewers; but the preacher sees his audience face-to-face. He hears their laughter, marks their tears, gauges their response. He is rewarded immediately by their attention.

It can be demonstrated over and over again that one who takes the trouble to prepare, who takes the pains to excel, can still draw a crowd. It has been well said that "the halcyon days of Christianity have always been the days of the right kind of preaching. All the decadent days of Christianity have been the days of the wrong kind of preaching." People cry out to us as they did to prophets of old, "Is there any word from the Lord?" They cry not out of curiosity but out of deep need. He who answers with words of purely human wisdom will fail them. He who seeks the real questions of life and offers the Bible's answers will not find his pews empty very long.

The value of preaching is seen in the fact that both the forerunner and the Savior chose it as their method.

The importance of preaching is challenged today — challenged openly. It is challenged not by enemies of the church but by its friends, challenged not by men in the pews but by men in the pulpits.

The very practitioners of our art have lost faith in its effectiveness. Some are far more concerned about what happens in the classrooms and in the counseling room than they are about what happens in the sanctuary. They are wrong, of course; and time will prove them wrong. Every generation has had its fads, and there will no doubt be new novelties in years to come. Across the years, preaching will remain, coming back again and again to claim its central place. Over the long haul, nothing will ever match the beauty of the feet of those that preach the gospel of peace.

Let us not forget that a single sermon, a poor one at that, converted Charles Spurgeon. Sangster was blessed, he said, for twenty years by a sermon he had heard. One of Moody's sermons changed the life of Wilfred Grenfell. One sermon by Charles G. Finney brought the Chief Justice of the Court of Appeals of the State of New York to the front seat. The sermons of Niemoeller and Bonhoeffer and Ludwig Steil so threatened Hitler that their mouths had to be stopped. They were lighting fires like those that Savonarola had — from his pulpit — kindled in Florence so long ago. Our sermons are not straws in the wind. The sound of our voices is not lost in the night. Cowper was right when he said that "while the world shall stand" the pulpit must stand as "the most important and effectual guard of truth."

Sangster is right when he says, "On his way to preach the gospel the most modest man may whisper to himself, 'Nothing more important will happen in this town this week than the work I am about to do.'"

Spurgeon's influence has reached farther and lasted longer than Queen Victoria's. Luther made a deeper impression on Germany than Charles V. Mary, Queen of Scots, said to John Knox, "I perceive that my subjects shall obey you and not me." England would have lost but little if George III had died in infancy, but the whole nation would have been impoverished if the infant John Wesley had not been rescued from the flames of the burning rectory at Epworth. Two centuries later we may still say with George Whitfield, "The Christian world is in a dead sleep. Nothing but a loud voice can wake the people out of it."

Look at the average congregation. Here is a man who is an alcoholic. He is trying desperately to break the habit. He is not succeeding very well. There is a couple who is living together "without the benefit of clergy." They have different mailing addresses, but that is about it. Here is a man who is dying. I know it and he knows it. There is a man who is getting a kickback from his firm's suppliers. It is bothering his conscience. I do not know if he's still doing it or not. There is a young man who is having an affair with a girl at work. His wife sits beside him. She knows nothing about it — only he and I know. There is a young mother, still in her twenties. She has just buried her husband and is left with three children to raise. Here is a man who believes everybody is against him. He thinks he does not have a friend in the world. There is a man whose wife is a hypochondriac. She feigns illness and he must care for her, even though he knows nothing is wrong.

What an opportunity! There is nothing like it in the whole community! No man — not the physician, not the attorney, not the teacher, not even the mayor — no man has the opportunity the preacher has.

Look at that congregation again! There sits the banker. Touch his life and I touch the world of finance. Here is a teacher. Affect her and I affect education. There is a physician. Influence him and I influence the world of medicine. There is the employee. Through him I speak to labor. Over there is the employer. Through him I speak to business. There is the man active in politics. Touch him and I touch government. There sits the attorney. Through him the field of law comes under my influence, too. Indeed, there is no sphere of human activity on this earth that is not under the influence of my pulpit. What an opportunity!

In the center of London beside a great cathedral is a marker at the spot where stood St. Paul's cross. That outdoor pulpit lasted from 1116 to 1613. Think of it! For five hundred years a pulpit stood in the heart of London! For far longer than that a pulpit has stood in the heart of the church. Preaching is central to worship, central to the church, central to Christianity. To put it in any other place is to ignore both Scripture and history.

Joseph Parker was once approached by a man who introduced himself by saying: "I am just an insignificant minister from Minnesota." Parker crisply answered, "There are no insignificant ministers of the Gospel of Jesus Christ."

"Where does great preaching begin?" a man asked. Someone said, "It begins where great rivers begin — in heaven." God is the fountainhead of great preaching. When we have to say with Thomas Chalmers, "My soul is losing acquaintance with God," then we must know that the rivers will soon dry up and the people pass over dry-shod. The cost of preaching is the cost of a deep devotional life.

For every one of us there is the danger that the flame will die out. What shall we do when our altars are cold, our lamps gone out, our faith no longer aflame? What if the burning heart becomes an ashen heart? It is the occupational hazard of the ministry that when we handle holy things they become commonplace and when they become commonplace they cease to be holy!

Lhamon says that the first essential to a great sermon is a great occasion. He adds, "The second essential to a great sermon is a great preacher. No man preaches taller than he is."

The apostle Paul said, "To the one we are the smell of death; to the other, the fragrance. And who is equal to such a task? Unlike so many, we do not peddle the word of God for profit. On the contrary, in Christ we speak before God with sincerity, like men sent from God" (2 Cor. 2:16, 17).

Chrysostom, already in his youth an accomplished rhetorician, rushed away and spent six years in lonesome study and devout meditation before he consented to enter the pulpit. Savonarola kindled his soul from the fires of Old Testament prophecy and from his pulpit kindled the fires of revolution in Florence. When him, preaching was so serious a business that when the papal agents sought to purchase his conscience with a cardinal's cap, he merely said that he expected a cap someday red with his own blood. Jonathan Edwards "was a man of faith and prayer, a man who handled the things that are unseen as things really seen and felt; a mind shining through a beautiful face...terribly in earnest, with a dreadful sense that sin was sin, Satan Satan, and Christ Christ."

A woman of the slums worshiped in George Matheson's congregation. She came to know, under his preaching, the power of the gospel. For a long time she

33

lived in a cellar, taking for granted that she could do no better. One day she astonished her neighbors by moving to a new place. She said, "You cannot hear George Matheson preach and live in a cellar."

How does a man manage to preach like that? He does not do it simply by condemning. We must do that, of course. John the Baptist did and so did Jesus. We miss our calling if we do not sometimes pronounce the woes of God's judgment. It is a poor sermon that is all diagnosis and no prescription. Hope and forgiveness are themes the world hears too little — and needs desperately to know. Have we, perhaps, traded the role of the shepherd for that of the sheepdog — nipping at the heels of the flock rather than leading them to higher ground? The *ecclesia* consists of those called out, not those driven out! We are called to joyfully announce good news, not mournfully relate bad news.

It is not that we ought to be like the speaker at the women's club who was introduced in this fashion: "This is Professor Smith, who is going to address us on Europe today; and she promises to leave out all the nasty things." There is no way to declare the whole counsel of God and leave out all the nasty things. It is, however, no gospel, no good news, that does not hold out a blessed hope, a forgiving love, an amazing grace.

Jowett once called on a cobbler in a little seaside town in England. The man worked alone in a very tiny room. Jowett asked him if he did not sometimes feel oppressed by the smallness of the chamber. "Oh, no," he said, and he opened a door that give him a glorious view of the sea.

For some who hear us preach, life has shrunken into an incredibly small room. They are confined and shut in by the narrowness of life. It is our privilege to open the door and let in the light. It is our joy to help them see the larger view — to help them see the image in which they were created and the destiny for which they were made.

"Light," cried the dying Goethe, "more light!" That is the cry of all humanity. Until the Light of the world comes into their lives in the person of Jesus, that cry will echo still. Only when men know him can we say, "The people walking in darkness have seen a great light; on those living in the land of the shadow of death, a light has dawned" (Isa. 9:2).

In the Pulpit

A sermon is not something that resides on paper. It can be argued that a written sermon is not really a sermon at all, just the record of one. The finest content will go unaccepted if the minister does not learn good delivery skills.

It is difficult to talk about delivery because it is so subjective. Whatever style a minister uses, he can find someone who likes it and someone who doesn't. It is also a matter of regional taste. What works in the south may not work in the north. What is warmly received in rural areas may be rejected in urban. Public speaking should resemble, but not be identical to ordinary conversation. It should be a more animated and structured version of ordinary conversation.

What are the basic principles of effective delivery?

First, *be natural*. This is a quality that is difficult to define. No one is totally natural behind the pulpit. Television has altered the kind of communicator best accepted. The modern communicator is expected to show warmth, humor and a moderate degree of transparency. The more at home you appear behind the pulpit, the more you will connect with an audience.

Secondly, *be enthusiastic*. This does not mean that you have to be loud and bombastic. It does mean that in some way, within your unique idiom, you convey that you care about your subject and the congregation.

Also, *be aware*. Have a sense of what is going on in

the congregation. Look at them. Scan the audience as you preach. You should be able to discern if you are getting through.

Finally, *be confident*. Believe in your ideas and abilities. Everyone is somewhat fearful, but it is the nervousness of a prize race horse, not the nervousness of a scampering mouse.

What method of delivery should you use?

You have several options. *You could use a complete manuscript.* This is not wise for most preachers. Not one man in a hundred can communicate effectively this way. This is not to say that you don't create a manuscript in the composition phase. That is highly recommended, but you don't take it into the pulpit. The preachers who use manuscripts well are those who don't even appear to look at it.

A better choice is an extended outline. This is an outline with some key ideas and illustrations written out in full. This offers some of the advantages of a manuscript without the drawbacks.

The most common method is probably the outline. This is the method where the sermon outline is reduced to as few pages as possible. This allows for maximum spontaneity without being impromptu.

More ministers should consider preaching without notes. The television stations use TelePrompTers so news anchors can appear to be speaking without notes. Politicians use them as well. The experts in the world of politics and communication know very well what communicates best. You don't have to memorize every line, just the outline. You take key words from your outline and attach to them items you already know through a peg system. The first few times you try this, you will want a backup outline in the back of your Bible. Most of you will never choose to try this. But, if you are looking for a little extra edge, this is a relatively easy way to get it.

Delivery is an integration of voice, facial expressions and body language.

We have to live with the voice we were given, but we can make some improvements. Try to find your natural pitch. Some preachers try to sound authoritative by pitching their voice too low. You can tell when you are doing that if you feel vibrations most pronounced in the throat. Some get excited and pitch their voice too high. They may not feel any vibrations at all. At your natural pitch you should feel the vibrations around the mask — the lips and chin. Much of good voice quality is a function of breathing from the diaphragm. When you breathe, your stomach should move out, your shoulders should not move up. Speak as if you had no microphone at all and let the people at the soundboard turn you down. Stay away from dairy products before you preach, and make sure your collar is not too tight.

Gestures should be as natural and unstudied as possible. If you are overusing a gesture, people will tell you. The best gestures are imitative, that is, they resemble the action in your story or exposition. Swaying from foot to foot is so common it is virtually epidemic. It can be discouraged by placing one foot slightly in front of the other. Move away from the pulpit if you wish, but do not pace like a caged animal.

Dress is an important consideration. While dress codes have relaxed a bit in modern society, most churches still expect to see their minister in a suit or at least a sport jacket and tie on Sunday morning. The boomer churches that allow the minister to go coatless and tieless are very rare. Even with the advent of casual dress at the office, many companies have had to specify what is acceptable. This has led to a new category of clothes called business casual. You will notice that while it is more casual than previous business dress, it is not as informal as regular casual. No matter how informal our own tastes, we still recognize dress codes. If you walked into an attorney's office and he was dressed in a

T-shirt and shorts, you would probably find a new attorney. Dress conservatively and in a way that does not draw attention away from the occasion to you.

Preaching that succeeds will be the marriage of substance and style. In our youth we often favor style. It is only later we come to truly appreciate the power of a dynamic idea. We don't have to choose one or the other. Manufacturers make quality products, but spend much time, money and energy on packaging. They would never offer a product with a hand lettered label. They want the package to reflect the quality of the product. That's why we are concerned both with quality content and quality delivery.

The glory of preaching is reflected in a story about Lorado Taft. The famous sculptor called his friends to the porch of his summerhouse to see the sunset. The western sky was ablaze with glory. As they marveled at the beauty of it, Mr. Taft spoke with such vivid language that the guest began to see the sunset through his eyes. All this time, the maid was standing by, unnoticed. Suddenly, she interrupted, "Mr. Taft, may I run down the road? I want to go home for a minute."

"Why do you want to go home at this particular moment?" Taft asked.

"I want to show Mother the sunset," she said.

"But your Mother has lived here a good many years," replied Mr. Taft. "She must have seen many sunsets."

"Oh, no," replied the maid. "We never saw the sunsets here until you came."

CHAPTER THREE

THE MINISTER AND DISCIPLESHIP

Since Jesus' *last* command to his followers was for them to make and mature disciples, those two tasks must be the *first* order of business for the church, for its leaders, and for the minister.

Making Disciples

One would suppose that making disciples (evangelism) begins with that Great Commission at the close of Jesus' earthly ministry. In fact, it begins much earlier. It begins in Eden. When Adam and Eve sinned, God did not say, "When things get difficult enough, they'll come running to me." No, God went to seek them. He called them by name. He asked them questions. And those are the first three elements of our evangelism. We must go to the lost, not wait for the lost to come to us. Jesus said that he came to *seek* and save that which was lost. We must know them well enough to call them by name. We must ask questions that will give them a chance to talk and give us a chance to determine the best approach.

The apostles followed Jesus' example. They went to Judea. They went to Samaria. They went to the uttermost parts of the earth. Remember Paul's dream of a man of

Macedonia saying, "Come over into Macedonia and help us"? You will recall that when Paul arrived in Macedonia, no one was waiting on the dock to meet him. As Alger Fitch wisely said, "It was not that Macedonia wanted Christ. It was that Christ wanted Macedonia."

Our evangelism cannot wait until people want Christ. Christ wants them. The Lord is not willing that any should perish. He wants all to come to repentance (2 Peter 3:9). Read also Psalm 96:3; Proverbs 11:30; Daniel 12:3; Matthew 4:19; Jude 23; John 20:21.

The first step is to find people to win. When you are the new minister in a place, visit in every home. In each place ask for the names of people they know who should be members of the church. Carry cards with you to write down the information. When you complete the rounds, you'll have a prospect list.

Most churches use attendance cards to get the names and addresses of visitors. Cards are more effective than the guest book. Certainly anyone who visits your service who is a local resident is likely to be a prospective member.

A more effective plan is to hand out cards on Sunday morning with a space marked for name, address, phone number and helpful information. Ask the congregation to give you the names of people who should be members of this church. They will think they know no one. You must help them. Suggest they think of relatives, friends, neighbors, co-workers in the office or factory, schoolmates and people with whom they do business. Be specific. "Who cuts your hair? Who is your insurance agent? Who services your car?" etc., etc. Only if you mention in detail these categories will they think of people who need to be won. *Do this three Sundays in a row.* Tell them they can take the card home and bring it back if they are unsure of the address. This is the best source of prospective members. The relatives and friends of those already members will be the most productive class of prospects.

If all else fails, you can conduct a religious census in selected neighborhoods. This is not highly productive, but it will turn up some. Do whatever you must to get these names.

It is also useful to check the membership rolls and Sunday School rolls for people who have other family members not a part of the church. You will assume that if a man will not come to church for his wife, he will not come for you. That's a mistake. There are many dynamics involved in his refusing his wife's urging to attend that are not a part of your own efforts. He may do it for you when he would never do it for her. (For convenience I have used the masculine pronoun. You will sometimes find that it is the husband who attends or belongs and not the wife. But you will find that less often.)

The next step is to build a bridge of friendship. Hand pick a group of people to visit the prospects. Some will be leaders, but others will not. Many good leaders do not make good visitors. Many good visitors will never be leaders. Instruct them thoroughly. Tell them where to go, when to go and what to say when they get there. Have them report back to you by writing on the back of the assignment card you will give them. You need information like former church connection, job, hobbies, family, and who they know in the church.

No prospect should be visited more often than once a month and never visited twice by the same member. Most often visitors go in pairs, either couples, or two men or two women. Some give assignments on Sunday and let them visit at their convenience. This is the least effective. Cards are lost, visits are postponed. When visits are made at the most convenient time for the visitor rather than all at once, you lose the momentum and the inspiration of a team effort. Visiting on the same night, going out from the church and returning to it, will keep workers from becoming discouraged.

Many go every Monday night with light refreshments afterward when they return to the church. Some designate a week each month. The advantage is that some are always bowling or at lodge on Monday night.

Visitors will need a city map and a flashlight. Rainy nights are best. People stay at home on rainy nights — and they are impressed when visited on those nights. The visitors introduce themselves and say what church they represent. They ask questions, but don't write anything down until they leave and are in the car. They speak highly of the church, its music, its preaching, its many activities and helpful groups. They stay from 15 to 30 minutes. Thirty minutes is the maximum. Back at the church, these people report enthusiastically to one another on the success of their visits. Visits that do not turn out well are never verbally shared with other visitors! Only upbeat verbal reports are allowed.

When just beginning your calling program, tell your people these are cultivation calls. They need not try to convert or instruct people. If a doctrinal question comes up, they should say, "I think our preacher can explain that better than I can. I'll ask him to contact you." At some point, however, you will want to institute a training class so that your team members can deal with many of these questions themselves. Not only does this better prepare them for the calling ministry, but it gives them the tools to deal with such situations which may arise in their everyday lives. Your members should never be too proud, however, to say "I don't know, but I'll find out," to any question a seeker may ask.

Of course, all this time you are visiting too. It's best to give the workers the better prospects and you take the more difficult ones. People will visit *with* you. They will not visit *for* you. You must be there every visitation night and you must go out every visitation night. Many ministers take their wives. If you have a woman without a partner, she can go with that woman. If you have a man without a partner, you will go with him. If everybody has a partner, you and your wife will visit together.

When you recruit these workers, tell them that this will be the happiest time of their Christian lives. They will get more out of the program than anyone else. There is no joy like the joy of soul winning.

When you visit, you will discuss any doctrinal matters that need explaining. It is good always to begin on common ground. If you are visiting a Catholic, you might begin by saying, "Everything you were taught in the Catholic Church about Jesus Christ we also believe and teach. Obviously we do not see eye to eye on the subject of Mary or on the doctrine of the church, but when it comes to Jesus Christ, we agree."

You can adapt this to other traditions. We have something in common with Methodists (prayer), Baptists (immersion), Presbyterians (church organization) and with most others. If you begin on common ground, you have a better climate for teaching on other significant themes.

For those with no church background at all you have a great opportunity to speak of undenominational Christianity and the privilege of being just a Christian.

After two cultivation visits by members and one visit by you, prospects are usually ready for a decision call. Teach your people how to do this. It is so easy. After a few introductory remarks about the church and its importance, they are asked to make a decision. The four magic words are, "Will you do it?" When you ask, wait for an answer. If you have a couple, the wife is a Christian, the husband is not, your calling partner must get her out of the conversation. When silence comes after your question, she will jump in with some remark that will spoil the moment. So you need two visiting together. One makes small talk with the party that is already a Christian so that the other can lead the prospect to a decision.

When you get an answer, it will usually be an excuse. People have two reasons: the presenting reason and the real reason. It is useful to ask, "In addition to that isn't

43

there some other reason?" Often then you will get to the real reason.

Most of the time when they give an excuse, you can say, "That's the very reason you ought to do it!"

For example: If the person says, "I'm not good enough," you can say, "That's the very reason you ought to do it. Often we sing, 'Just as I am,' at invitation time. Nobody is good enough, but if we give God a chance, he will make us better than we are and we will grow. Will you do it?"

Perhaps the person says, "I want to think about it." Your answer is, "No one should do this thoughtlessly. In fact my guess is you have thought about it for a long time — and you and I have had a chance to think about it together tonight. So really, now is the time for action. Will you do it?"

Wait for an answer. The longer you wait, the greater the odds are that the answer will be YES. Do not give up until your four magic words have been asked three times. If you don't get a YES then, say you hope they'll change their mind and that you will be praying that they will.

Is this pressing too hard? No. People are lost. Someone must feel a sense of urgency about it. They don't, so you must.

Often the Bible tells us to persuade people (Acts 2:40; 1 Tim. 6:2; 2 Tim. 4:2; Titus 1:9). Persuasion is not manipulation. Manipulation is trying to get a person to do something for the wrong reason. Persuasion is trying to get them to do something for the right reason. Do not be afraid to persuade. The harder it is to win a person, the harder it is to lose them later. The easier it is to win them, the easier it is to lose them later.

Some preachers have had success with an Inquirer's Clas, taught by the minister, and running for about six weeks at the usual Sunday School hour. Some arrange to always be at the church on a certain night, and visitors are invited to come to the church to learn more in a personal conference with the preacher. Others have held Visitor Dinners which include a nice menu, good music, information about the various activities of the church and a *brief* talk by the preacher about the church and its doctrine. If you have a large number of prospective members this may work for you.

When a person comes forward at the invitation who has not made a profession of faith, you should ask them to repeat after you, "I believe that Jesus is the Christ, the Son of the living God." If they have previously made a profession of faith, you should ask them to repeat after you, "I *still* believe that Jesus is the Christ, the Son of the living God."

For those to be baptized, baptism should occur when practicable. You will need to select a couple to assist at baptisms. They need not be leaders. Often it is a couple who has no other task. They should be kind, helpful and self-assured. They will show candidates where the baptismal garments are and answer any questions they have.

For women you should have four sizes of baptismal robes. They should be of a material heavy enough that it does not cling when wet. Have someone in the church sew fishing sinkers into the hem so it will hang properly even when wet. Most of them are designed with an oversize collar that makes an X across the front and ties in the back. For men have someone make pajama type trousers and a long white coat like a doctor wears. The baptismal assistants are familiar with these garments.

Most of the time candidates will be asked to bring a change of underclothing, but you should have a few sets around in case of unanticipated decisions. You should also have plenty of towels and handkerchiefs.

It is important for people to witness baptisms. It is the most sacred part of worship, but since they often occur at the end of a service of worship, some people slip out before the baptism. This can be kept to minimum if the baptismal service is streamlined. Long delays discourage people from waiting for this part of the service. Send the candidates to the dressing rooms with the couple and announce a baptismal hymn, emphasizing that they will sing one verse. That signals that there will not be a long period of preparation. As soon as you are backstage take off your jacket and step into the baptismal waders. You will need to purchase them, and a minister's baptismal robe, from a church supply house. Quickly roll up your shirt sleeves. Your assistant immediately holds the robe for you to slip into it. Fasten it as you go down the steps into the baptistery. Your presence will reassure the audience that there will not be a long delay. If the candidates are not quite ready, you can say a few words, quote a verse or two of Scripture, and then you should offer prayer. Help the candidate down the steps. Direct him or her to the end of the baptistery. If you are right handed, have the person stand at your right side with the person between you and the congregation.

Most modern baptisteries have some means to heat the water. If the water is warm it helps the candidate to relax.

Almost all ministers repeat the words from the great commission "in the name of the Father, and of the Son and of the Holy Spirit." Some add a few words that further explain baptism. If you become confused or leave something out, do not worry about it. We do not believe in magic words. It is the intent of the person that makes baptism valid, not the precise words you speak.

It is not a pretty sight to see someone holding his nose as he is about to be baptized. Take a clean handkerchief and have the person hold it in his right hand. Put his left hand underneath (behind) that one and then your own left hand (assuming you are right handed.) In this way an arm cannot flail out and splash at the water or grab the side of the baptistery. Place your right hand behind the person's neck and lower them slowly into the water. Here is where many ministers make a mistake. They think they must move quickly because the person is holding his breath. But if you lower them quickly they will think you have dropped them. It is better to lower them slowly. In fact, you cannot go too slowly. As you lower them, you walk toward the person's head. When you are ready to immerse them, the head is right in front of you, not at the end of an extended arm. If the candidate is much taller than you, instruct him or her to bend their knees after you say AMEN. With many men and boys you must sometimes say, "Don't try to help me. Let me do it."

Many people, especially women, float easily and you will have to push them down into the water with your left hand.

Then raise them up and give them a minute to catch their breath. Guide them toward the steps, stepping between them and the congregation in case you need to shield them from view.

After the baptism ask someone to lead a closing prayer. Ask someone who does not normally pray short prayers. Leave the baptistery removing your robe as you go up the steps. The robe you order will have a zipper. Disregard that and have someone sew snap fasteners on the robe. Then you can simply grasp it at the top and pull it apart all the way down. Your assistant has already guided the candidate to the robing room and stands ready to lift your robe off you. Then step out of the waders and into your shoes. Don't worry about unrolling your sleeves. Just put on your jacket and you're ready to greet worshipers.

Never joke with the candidate before or after baptism. It is a solemn ceremony. It depicts the central facts of our faith: Christ's death, burial and resurrection. It is a solemn occasion.

Sometimes you will have a person who wants to be baptized in running water. There is no reason you should object to this. Try to check out the place before-hand. Baptize them with the head going upstream. Make sure you have firm footing before you immerse them. Have someone ready to put a blanket around them as they emerge from the stream.

You will sometimes have opportunity to baptize an invalid. A home bathtub works well for this. It may be that the lower half of the body will come out of the water as the upper half goes under. That's not important. You have immersed them.

Evangelism goes beyond the local church. It also involves a commitment to world missions. As the preacher, you have a key role to play in the congregation's attitude toward and support of missions. No church is healthy that is completely preoccupied with the local scene. Every congregation must have a heart for world evangelism. It is part of your job to help create this attitude.

First, you must encourage giving to missions. Whether the church has a Missions Fair, Missions Conference, Faith Promise Weekend or some other plan, you should support it. While much of the planning will be in the hands of a committee or task force, you should also be involved. If all you give is moral support, that is significant. You will help them select the dates, suggest possible speakers, and use the pulpit to focus attention on missions.

It may be that missions is a part of the general budget of the church. If so, you will likely discover some degree of tension between the financial committee and the missions committee. Often the finance committee thinks that all the money given to missions is wasted. The missions committee is likely to think that all the money is wasted *except* that which is given to missions. The missionary dollar is no more or less sacred than the dollar devoted to church growth and evangelism at home. You will need to create a balance between the local and distant needs.

You will also have a role in helping the church decide which missionary cause to support. You do not decide for them, but you do advise and consent. There may be worthy missionaries or causes you could encourage them to support. There may be unworthy ones you will subtly encourage them to drop. Usually, someone in the church will have a favorite mission. Sometimes a relative of theirs is part of the endeavor. You may need to be diplomatic in such situations. Better to give some money to a missionary who is marginally effective and keep peace, than to opt for efficiency and lose more than you gain.

You will be better acquainted with these causes than most. You have a real opportunity to guide and you should. But, no one should feel you are dictating missionary policy or that you are single-handedly deciding where the missionary dollar goes.

Maturing Disciples

Everyone knows that there is a second half to the Great Commission; that we are to teach people to observe all things that Jesus commanded. So we must have a good program of follow-up after evangelism.

Make a checklist and ask your secretary (or a volunteer if you have no secretary) to be certain each new member is put on the mailing list and receives a new member packet hand delivered to the home. In the packet will be some biblical leaflets, a copy of the church membership directory, a copy of the church budget and a set of offering envelopes. The time to teach stewardship is at the very beginning.

It has been demonstrated that new members who do not become part of a small group within six months are likely to leave the church. Alert the proper Sunday School class and see if the new member can be enrolled in Sunday School. Other small groups include the choir, the ladies circle, the men's fellowship, the youth group, a ministry team, a committee, or service as a greeter or usher.

New Member classes have been widely tried, but with little success. This is due in part to the fact that some new members already belong to a Sunday School class, and also due to the wide age difference in a group of new members.

What is your role in the Sunday School? Depending on the size of your congregation, be ready to "advise and consent" on all teacher appointments. You may know things that others do not; things you may not be able to tell. You know reasons that a person should not teach, and you know people with talent and character. No teacher should be appointed without the knowledge of a minister. In a smaller church this would probably be you. In most larger churches, the Minister of Education would take on this task. The exception is that any teacher should be free to secure a substitute or a special speaker for just one Sunday. But regular substitutes, assistant teachers and regular teachers should have your approval.

Should you yourself teach class? It's hard to say. There are two good reasons for doing so. One is that you're are the most qualified. The other is that people will attend your class who otherwise would not come to Sunday School at all. It is partly a matter of prestige, and partly the fact that they think you are knowledgeable. There are two reasons for not teaching. One is that you may not be able to separate your sermon from your lesson. And if you have more than one morning service you may need the time to rest. You will have to decide this based on your own local situation.

There will also be other classes, perhaps on Wednesday nights. You will be expected to teach and you should.

The distribution of good Christian periodicals and other literature is another way to help disciples mature.

Most churches have a church library. It is the least visited room in the building and the church librarian is the loneliest person in the congregation. Some churches put good books on a tea cart and park it in the foyer where everybody has to pass it. In this way they encourage use of the church library.

From time to time you will want to design a program to build attendance, either in Sunday School or morning worship. While there are many variations to these campaigns, they will all need these factors if they are to succeed:

1. A clear reachable goal.
2. People definitely recruited to do the work, who have definite assignments.
3. A catchy slogan or theme.
4. Good advertising by means of pulpit announcements, the church newsletter, letters mailed to the constituency, posters and possibly a theme song, a children's poster contest, a skit, or some means to dramatize the effort. A good rule is that anything must be announced at least three Sundays and advertised in at least three ways.
5. No campaign should be open ended. It should have a definite time to begin and a definite time to end.
6. Every campaign should end on a positive note, even if the results were less than expected. The workers should be praised and rewarded. Some object to that. But they are wrong. It is not that people work *for* the praise or *for* the reward. It is rather that courtesy demands we say Thank You to faithful workers — and it will be easier to recruit workers next time if they are properly recognized this time.

Church Growth

We know that Jesus intended the church to grow. When he spoke of the church as a body, or a vine, or a household, all those pictures suggested growth. The apostle Paul wrote that the church should grow. There are many good books on church growth, and you should read several of them.

The subject is too large for a few paragraphs, but these

51

facts seem to be generally accepted. The church grows when it is sensitive to the needs of people in the community and moves to meet those needs effectively. You should find some community need that no other church is addressing *and* for which there are gifted people in your congregation. It may be a deaf ministry, a ministry to the blind, a ministry to the poor, it may be directed at teens or children, or families with special difficulties. It may be adult literacy, or helping disabled people, or children with learning problems. It may be working with alcoholics or drug dependent people or single parents or divorced people. God has already put in the congregation you serve people with skills and the desire to serve. Match them with the need, and you are on the way. The church must meet these needs effectively and serve the target group so well that the congregation is known in the community. Why is this important? Because today we must earn the right to be heard. People will not listen to our doctrinal lessons until we have shown that we have a caring heart. Then they will listen.

You can get from the Chamber of Commerce, or the Farm Bureau if you serve a rural church, a survey showing the demographics of the community. It will help you know what kind of people live there and help you select a target group. You serve everyone. You want to win everyone. But you design programs that target specific groups.

However, do not be dismayed if the community is not growing. There are many growing churches in stagnant 'communities, and many stagnant churches in growing communities.

Church growth begins with attendance building. Special days can help. The Sunday after a special campaign attendance will drop, but you will have introduced several new people to your church. In a year or two, your special day attendance can become your normal attendance. Christmas and Easter lend themselves to attendance promotion. It makes no sense to try to promote a big attendance when the attendance is normally down. Take advantage of the stronger attendance patterns of spring and fall. Take advantage of the tendency people show to want to go to church at Christmas and Easter. It might be good to schedule a big attendance day a Sunday or two before Easter. That way, those who were introduced to your church and liked it are also likely to come on Easter. While Sunday School has fallen on hard times, a Back to Sunday School Day is still profitable. Founders Day, Anniversary Sunday or Homecoming will still bring out a crowd. Remember though, you cannot have a big day by just announcing it. You must have a plan and you must have promotion. A low-key way to increase attendance is to coordinate your effort with a sermon series. In January you might have a series entitled, "Four Recipes for a Happy New Year." Near Easter you might have a series on "Walking with Jesus." Promote the series with flyers or bulletin inserts.

Location is extremely important. The church building needs to be visible and accessible. If the building lacks visibility then the members must be highly visible in the community — and you must be highly visible in the community. Its programs, activities and visitation can help overcome a bad location.

In addition to programs to meet needs, we show that we care by visitation. Visitation by members is more effective than your visitation because it is assumed that that is your job. When members visit, it says, "We care about you." That does not mean that you can just let them visit. They will not visit unless you visit, and your visiting fills in gaps that they as amateurs cannot fill. But if both you and the members visit in homes and offices it will help the church to grow.

Good music is an important component of church growth. It really is not so important what kind of music as it is that the music be done well. Know your community. Find out what radio stations they listen to.

Then you will know the type of music they prefer. Whatever type it is, it should be done well.

Programs and activities are essential to church growth, but people attract people to church. Programs and activities will keep them coming once they have started, but you must begin with people.

As the church grows, power shifts. Instinctively, people realize this and may actually oppose growth. However, they cannot keep you from visiting, nor your chosen workers from visiting. They cannot keep new members from coming. Every growing church has a few in it who wish the church would stay the same. They cannot really block growth if you resolve to work around them.

Advertising has its place, but there is a saying that a lot of advertising does a little good, while a little advertising does no good at all. Ads in the local paper and in the phone book are essential. Billboards are great. The lovely printed folders that most churches produce do little *unless* accompanied by a program for distribution and follow-up.

A nice sign on the church lawn advertising a Christmas Eve Service or Easter music will bring in visitors. Some people might think a "cantata" would be dull and highbrow. Instead, you might consider advertising "The Music of Easter" or "The Music of Christmas." People will come to that.

When an event is over take down the sign *immediately*. A sign advertising something that happened days or weeks ago says that the church is careless.

All exterior signs should be professionally done. Do not permit some amateur to make a sign. Insist that it be done professionally. A poor sign suggests that everything else you do will be done poorly. People must be able to read *everything* on a sign in three seconds or they will read *nothing* on the sign!

One of the easiest ways to advertise is to plant flowers around the sign and around the church building. That catches the eye, and costs little. Because flowers change with the seasons, people will begin to really "see" the building. What we see all the time we never see at all unless it changes. That's why shopping centers completely remodel every ten years. You can't do that, but you can change flowers and shrubs; and paint is cheap. Keep the exterior and interior of the property painted and clean. Keep the lawn mowed and the bushes trimmed.

Parking is essential. Visitors don't come early. Members do. They get the best spaces and assume there is no parking problem. But if a visitor cannot see readily where to park, he or she will go on to some other church. A parking attendant can help if it is not someone who sees himself as a policeman. Rather he should see himself as a helpful greeter.

You may need to use off-site parking, encourage your faithful to park there, and even provide a shuttle. Visitors will not hunt for a place to park. It doesn't matter how many seats you have in the building if the people can't find a place to park their car.

Friendliness ought to begin in the parking lot. A greeter should casually welcome people right there. Other greeters should be at the door. Don't put a badge or ribbon on them. That makes their greetings look perfunctory. Let it appear that they are just friendly members. In each section of the sanctuary have a secret host. That person greets everyone in that section, especially those he or she does not know.

Asking visitors to stand and introduce themselves embarrasses many people, especially those we want the most to win. It is fine to welcome the visitors and draw their attention to the visitor card and even to hand out a visitor packet, but don't make them stand and introduce themselves. Some churches have adopted the policy of having the *members* stand. This allows those sitting near visitors to take note of them and shake their hand without making them feel they have been put on public display in front of a large crowd.

It has been demonstrated that if visitors are visited in their homes by a member of the church within 36 hours, 85% will return for a second visit. And those who are second time visitors are real prospects for regular attendance and membership.

The keeping of accurate attendance records is essential. A head count should be taken at every service. Keep a chart with the monthly averages in your desk. You can compare this month with last month, or this month with the same month last year. Keep a running total of membership. Add new members to it and delete those who die, move away, or move their membership to another church. Then you will know in an instant if you have a net gain, and you will never guess as to the number of members.

There are always those who want to cull the membership rolls and drop those who are inactive. This is an exercise in futility. It accomplishes nothing. In fact, if 90% of the members are active you are in trouble. There is no one to work on for attendance growth. If 50% of the members are active you have a field in which to work. Admittedly, it is easier to win five new members than to reactivate one who has become inactive. Still, they are your responsibility until they take the initiative to remove their names. Of course you will keep a resident membership roll and a nonresident membership roll. Some even have an active and an inactive roll. But don't waste time (and hurt feelings) by culling out those members somebody thinks have become inactive.

What do you do when the congregation has grown to the point that space is a problem? More people attend Sunday morning worship than any other service, so the emphasis should be on an attractive and comfortable place to worship. You can be more creative as to where to put a Sunday School class or a small group than you can where to have worship. A common solution and a good one is to go to two services. That is a lot less

56

expensive than building a whole new facility. Many people will resist this at first. They will say that they cannot know everyone in the church. The problem with their logic is, they can't know everyone in the church in one service. Moving to two services takes careful planning. A common choice is two worship services with a Sunday School in between. Some churches do simultaneous multiple worship and Sunday School. This takes even more planning and will not help if you have a shortage of parking. Most churches who go to two services report an increase in attendance because they have added to the number of choices. A church is considered full at 75-80% of seating capacity. People don't like to crowd into pews and sit close to strangers. Don't always rely on an architect's estimate of seating capacity. Architects must think all churchgoers are very thin and like each other very much. It is best if your early service is not earlier than 8:30. The last service should be no earlier than 10:30, and 11:00 is probably better. Many people love to sleep late on Sundays. Would that we all have enough growth that we have to struggle with these problems.

CHAPTER FOUR

THE MINISTER AS ADMINISTRATOR

Administration is an essential part of the minister's job. Many rate it as their least favorite activity. Many who enter ministry are people persons and would rather sit on the porch and talk than do detail work. Others love to work on brochures and flow charts and never come into contact with a human being. You don't need to be an excellent administrator to be a successful minister, but you do need to be adequate. What is adequate? Whatever it takes to fulfill the job you have been called to do. Some people define administration as paperwork, but it is just as much people work.

Minister's Relationships with Elders and Deacons

Churches vary widely in how they organize themselves for business. Some have a joint board of elders and deacons for mainly business matters and an elders' meeting for consideration of spiritual matters, personnel matters, benevolence, shepherding and strategic planning. In some cases this works quite well. Some churches are now experimenting with a ministry leaders' system, where deacons, or people like them, do not meet in a joint board, but run a ministry under the supervision of the elders. When one minister was asked what he thought about the ministry system he said, "Aren't they committees under a different name?" There does seem to be more to it than that.

The benefits to the old system include a sense of camaraderie and participation on the part of the leadership, and the deacons spend time learning from the elders. The drawback is that in some cases the elders and deacons become political enemies, and the deacons, who are generally younger and more inexperienced, can outvote the elders. An additional problem is determining what is a business matter and what is a spiritual matter. If there is mutual respect and understanding of the biblical roles, then a joint board operating well need not be replaced.

The advantage to the ministry system is that more opportunity is given to members of the congregation to actually utilize their gifts. The disadvantage of the system is that not every good servant is endowed with the organizational skills to lead a ministry. Another drawback is the incredible amount of administration it takes to keep the program together. The biggest problem noted is that individuals in churches moving to the ministry system often see it as a power grab by the elders. This is not necessarily the case, but it is frequently perceived that way. Ministry leaders have a lot of authority in their own ministry area, but do not have any outside it. It gives them more power, but in a narrower field. It is not our purpose to tell you which system to choose.

Don't change for the sake of change. The main things to ask are, "Is the work getting done and are the roles being fulfilled?" The Bible gives us a general outline and we are free to adapt it within the structure of the Scriptures.

When the committees, or ministry teams, are appointed each year, you should be involved. You know the congregation better than anyone else. You know the competent people who are not well known by the congregation at large. You also know about personal problems that might make it unwise to give a certain person a certain responsibility. Usually the chairman of the elders, chairman of the deacons and you will have the primary influence over these appointments. Sometimes the board will ratify them. This would be particularly true under the ministry system. Committees, or ministry teams, should be allowed and even encouraged to add people to their teams.

Your list of leaders should be posted, or published, at the beginning of each year. It is probably not best to publish addresses and phone numbers by their names. People intent on trouble and chronic complainers may find this an easy course of action, thus discouraging your volunteers. If someone has a serious suggestion, he or she can find the person or look up the number.

Whatever system you are under, it is imperative that you develop a good working relationship with the chosen leaders. We will use the term "board" and you can fill in the rest according to whatever system your church uses.

The minister and the board should never view themselves as adversaries. This is one of the great tragedies of our times. Elders, deacons, trustees and ministers are arguing over who should set the church agenda. The best of all possible situations is one in which the board encourages leadership from the minister and the minister encourages guidance and input from the board. There are still a few churches who do not invite the minister to elders' meetings. This is a great mistake. How can they operate efficiently if they do not meet together?

Some of these problems might be avoided if the board and minister would meet for fellowship, study or prayer apart from the business meetings. One minister had the board come over to his house every Monday night to watch Monday night football. There was no grand design other than to get to know each other better.

A minister should acknowledge board members in public. At least the minister gets paid for his troubles. Board members serve with no financial blessing and little encouragement. One way to encourage the board is to have a significant ordination or installation service. This says to the congregation that the leaders are worthy of honor.

It is great for a board to have a yearly planning and/or training session. A retreat would be a good environment. Start with whatever time the church will give you. Start with a morning session at church then move to a meeting room at the mall. Finally, you can go to a camp or conference center and stay overnight. The sessions not only allow for planning, but they can also build camaraderie.

Another helpful strategy is to change by adding, not subtracting. This rule can be applied several ways. Don't cancel existing classes, add a new one. Don't take a person's job away from them (apart from gross mismanagement). Create a new job and find a new volunteer.

Another good piece of advice for the minister is, "Don't play favorites." That is, resist the tendency to favor those who generally support your agenda.

Many ministers report great resistance from the board toward any idea they share. Every board will react differently. Boards are notoriously quirky when it comes to making decisions. One meeting, they may argue the entire meeting over the price of crayons and the next week spend only five minutes on a new air conditioning system. Still, there are some helpful strategies for sharing your ideas.

One minister used to advise younger ministers to, "Plant ideas like seeds, not bullets." What did he mean by this? You, as the minister, have perhaps spent hours coming up with an idea and refining it. You might have over ten hours of thinking time, or more, in the proposal. The problem is, you want the board to process the material in ten minutes. We need to give them some time to have the same privilege we had to think about the project.

Why not produce a written proposal with the words "Discussion Draft" printed across the top? This suggests you are not too proud to accept revisions to your idea. It is sometimes wise to present a proposal at one meeting and not ask for a decision. You then have a month for the board members to consider the project and for you to make your case.

Don't be discouraged if every idea is not accepted. This does not mean you are a failure. No leader, however great, has every idea accepted. Don't be discouraged if an idea is altered. Often, the board will think of things you did not think of. Often they will suggest improvements. Their participation in the decision making enhances the possibility of their support.

Don't make every idea you share a test of wills. Some ministers approach each proposal as a battle where there must be a winner and loser.

Another way to get a hearing for good ideas is to let the leaders participate in brainstorming sessions. A board and the staff should have a retreat from time to time where they can dream as if price were no object. Sometimes a board member will suggest a program that the minister could support with enthusiasm. Sometimes a program is perceived differently when it is proposed by a board member rather then a minister.

One other piece of advice: Don't ask permission to do routine or maintenance items. This is not a power issue, it is an effectiveness issue. Should board meeting time be wasted to talk about replacing a light bulb or repainting the sign when the service times change? The board should entrust the senior minister with enough authority to make these routine decisions. They may want to set some price limit to what expenditures the minister can authorize from the budget without specific board permission. This would save an enormous amount of time. What about inviting missionaries? They usually call the minister to ask about coming to speak. By the time we refer it to various committees and bring it up for a vote, they are already back on the field. Consider setting a policy concerning how many and what kinds of missions a minister may invite for a given year. The same could be done for singing groups.

What do you do when a committee or ministry team does not function? Don't scold them. Suggest to the leader some things you would like them to take up at the next meeting. Ask him when the next meeting will be and ask if it is possible to get such and such done by a given date. You may want to attend the meeting. Try to work with the ministry team. If that fails, you have to work around them to get the job done.

Having a committee or leadership team does not absolve you of responsibility. For instance, even though you have a building and grounds committee or ministry team, you need to be alert to broken windows, peeling paint, worn carpets, faded signs, overgrown shrubbery and the like. Our members are busy people. They may come regularly on Sunday and get used to the way things look. The longer we look at repairs that need to be fixed, the more we get used to them. One congregation divided the property into three sections and repainted one third of the rooms and buildings each year. That spread the cost and kept the property looking fresh.

Board Meetings

Many ministers have related to the statement of the preacher who said, "If I die and wake up in a board meeting, I'll know I've gone to Hell."

How can we bring a little Heaven into our meetings?

First, *start on time.* Waiting for folks to arrive just rewards them for being late. Soon, everyone will start showing up late because they know the meeting will not start on time.

Also, you should *end on time.* Endless meetings also breed absenteeism. Many a tense meeting would have been avoided if it had not dragged on until midnight. People do not think well when exhausted. The meeting should have an end time and it should be observed.

Have a printed agenda. It is not wise to conduct a meeting by going around the room and asking what each person thinks. That is a prescription for long hours and tense meetings.

Take attendance. It shows that service to the board is considered a priority in your church.

Don't do committee work during the meeting. A particularly vexing problem can be assigned to a committee, ministry or task force. There, those who are truly interested can hammer out a solution.

Let everything be done in openness and love. You will not be able to control what other people do, but you can set an example.

Don't get sidetracked. Let people talk about football and politics after the business is concluded. You can schedule a coffee time afterwards to have fellowship and conversation.

Everyone should back the decision once it is made. What does this mean? Does it mean we require someone to be dishonest about his opinion or vote? No. Nor does this mean that someone who opposed the program should become the point man for it. He should, however, not criticize the outcome publicly or privately. If someone comes to the board member, he might say something like, "We worked hard in the board meeting to come up with a solution. This was the product of our best efforts, and we all need to get behind it."

A side issue, but still an important one, concerns

what the minister should do when his salary is being discussed. Generally, ministers should be absent during salary discussions, but should be allowed to first make their case. You probably have a right to be there, but exercising your rights is not always productive. People have a right to oppose your raise without appearing to oppose you. Some genuinely believe the church can't afford it. Let them express their opinion without spoiling their relationship with their shepherd. A senior minister should stay when the staff salaries are discussed so he can be an advocate for them. Do let the board know what your overhead is. They often forget how much you spend on travel and that you will often be paying your own health insurance and retirement. Often they compare their net with your gross.

The minister may not be able to have a huge impact on how meetings are run. We must always remember we are working with volunteers. Still, from time to time you can meet with your chairman and help him help the board to have better meetings.

The Minister and His Staff

Other than moral failure, nothing has so broken churches as dissension in the ministerial staff. Certainly there is fault on both sides.

First, consider things from the junior minister's perspective. Often a junior staff member is impatient with what he regards as the senior minister's deficiencies. He dreams of how he might do things better if he were in charge. No minister is competent in all areas. An associate needs to accept the senior minister's weaknesses, just as he hopes his will be tolerated. Since a junior staff member is usually younger, he may be at the most idealistic time of his life. He is filled with ideas from Bible College or Seminary. He knows how things should work on paper. He is anxious to prove his mettle. The senior minister often has a more realistic idea about what is possible. Sometimes, if there is a faction opposed to the senior minister, they will stroke the junior staff member's ego. They will tell him he preaches better than the senior minister or that he would be a better leader. While this might be true, most often they are simply trying to gain an ally. While the following advice may not be warmly welcomed by associates, it is important. If you can't be loyal to your senior minister — you leave! Don't get involved in a coup against him. People who will involve you in a coup may someday lead one against you. For good or ill, the board, and maybe even God, has placed the senior minister in that position. As such, he is the senior staff member. He is the boss.

Senior ministers are also guilty of complicating staff relationships. Often they struggle with finding the balance between oversupervising or ignoring the junior staff. The most common complaint from associates is that the senior minister wants to use them as an errand boy. Others say the senior minister criticizes them in public. Whenever possible the senior minister should support the associate. He should fight for his financial well-being. He should not be quick to abandon him for some small offense.

Staff members do not have to be the best of friends. If they are too close, they might have a lot of fun, but get little work done. The two indispensable qualities are trust and respect. With those two present, you don't necessarily need to socialize outside the working environment.

The senior minister must be the chief of staff. Every employee has a right to know to whom he answers. Churches become very complex in this regard. No person is better qualified or in a better position to manage the church staff. This includes ministerial, clerical and custodial staff. Of course, the minister answers to the board, just as a college president answers to the board of trustees and a CEO answers to the board of directors.

The Volunteer Staff

No congregation can do its work without volunteers. Securing volunteers and keeping them happily at work is essential. Ordinarily, you should not make public appeals for workers. You will get a limited response. Also, some may respond who mean well, but are not at all suitable for the job. This is true even of such tasks as child care or driving the church van. Of course, if you are having a work day to clean the building or clean the grounds, you will feel free to ask for volunteers. But, before you ask for volunteers you will already have spoken personally with several workers so that you'll know you will have a good crew.

Child care, visitation, teaching, and communion preparation are all jobs that need to be filled in a different way. Unless the congregation is quite large, you should enlist them. For many tasks, you can enlist them over the telephone. But, if it is a very significant assignment, such as teaching a class or being a youth sponsor, you should go to the home or office and ask them to do the job. It is especially useful if you do not go alone. If the Bible School superintendent goes with you to recruit a teacher, if the Youth Minister goes with you to recruit a sponsor, you will have a higher degree of success. Tell them that there is a job you believe they can do well. Emphasize both the need and your confidence in their ability to do the job. Never ask people to do a job indefinitely. It may be for a year. In some cases it may be three months. Mention the end date when you ask them to volunteer. In this way they can be replaced without embarrassment at the end of the period. Tell them you will help them, or name some other leader who will help them. Tell them the church will provide what they need to do the job as long as it is within reason.

One youth minister used these techniques in a clever way. He invited select members of the church to his house for a spaghetti supper, which he cooked. He asked the members for their opinions on the kind of youth program they wanted. He separated them into groups to plan an ideal program. At the end of the session, he said that he valued their opinion and hoped they could volunteer to help. Not one member of the dinner party turned him down. Not all of them stayed with the program long term. That's all right. He had time to replace them. Over half stayed longer than two years.

At the beginning of each year, all volunteer jobs come up for renewal or replacement. Sometimes you will have to replace a person before the end of the time period. The person may not be doing the job, or not doing it properly. There may be personal problems that require a change. These must be handled with great care. First, find a replacement. Then go to the person and say something like, "We are trying to give some experience to our new workers, and at the same time give a rest to those who have worked hard and deserve it. Would you be willing to let John Doe step in for a while in your present responsibility? He has lots of ability, but he needs experience. If you would be willing to do that, we'd like you to take on a different and significant responsibility while we see how John works out in this job."

If that seems impossible, then give him or her an assistant. Confidentially advise the person that you need him or her to shoulder much of the load. It will take all your finesse to accomplish this. Do it only if it must be done. You are not lying. You may not be telling all you think or know, but what you say is the truth. Honesty requires us to tell the truth; it does not require us to tell all we know to be true.

Never scold a congregation because you don't have enough volunteers for child care or communion preparation or cleaning the church. People do not respond well to this approach. Handle these things behind the scenes if possible.

If your congregation is quite large, you will need a gifted volunteer to be Director of Volunteer Services. This should not be a paid position. Her or his role should be much like that of the lady who coordinates volunteers at the hospital. It will need to be a person with lots of personality, someone kind and patient, one to whom it is difficult to say, "No." You will work closely with this person. You may know good reasons why a person should not be given a specific job. You cannot tell why, but you only say to the Director of Volunteer services, "I think the time is not right for that person to do that job. I cannot say more than that."

Kennon Callahan, in his marvelous book, *Twelve Keys to an Effective Church*, says that you look first for competence then for compassion and then for commitment. We've often done it the other way — with poor results. We find committed people with abrasive personalities and marginal competence and wonder why they fail. You can lead people to deeper commitment. You can sometimes even help them become more compassionate. You cannot give them competence. Some will never be able to teach, or sing, or visit, or be a good greeter or usher. So begin with competent people. Show them by word and example the need to be compassionate. Lead them to deeper commitment. The very job you give them may be the springboard to deeper commitment.

The work of volunteers should be recognized from time to time. Once a year you may want to have a dinner to honor them, or you may want to recognize them in the morning worship service. You may want to commission them as they begin their work with an appropriate prayer in the service. Once or twice a year write a personal note to your volunteers. Tell them you appreciate what they do. Tell them how much it means to the work of the church. Too many teachers have been handed a book on Sunday morning, sent to the beginner department to teach and never been noticed again. People spend years caring for other people's babies and no one ever says, "Thanks, you are doing a good job." Musicians are especially ignored this way. If our Lord will say to us at the gates of heaven, "Well done, good and faith faithful servant," then it is surely good for us to say the same thing on earth.

The Minister and Conflict

A significant part of the minister's administrative duties involve dealing with people problems. Very few ministers have been fired because they didn't know enough about the Bible, but many have been because they could not get along with people.

Some ministers report the handling of criticism to be their number one problem. They should not feel alone. They aren't the only ones who deal with this. Any leader will have to face a great amount of second guessing. What about politicians? What about coaches? What about teachers? Criticism is the price of leadership.

Those who criticize can be grouped into four categories.

First, there is the Chronic Complainer. This person complains about everything, not just church matters. To them, complaining is like a hobby. This person is only an irritant. They are rarely dangerous.

The second person is the Impatient Visionary. This person means well. He really does want to see the church grow. The problem is he wants to see it now. You will probably like this person, at least at first. He will share'your desire for positive change. The difficulty arises when you and the church can't change fast enough for him.

The third complainer is the Traditionalist. This is another well-meaning person who see himself as the keeper of church tradition. To him, any change seems like a negative reflection on the past. He takes change as an insult.

The last and most dangerous complainer is the Power-

71

hungry Manipulator. This person has one goal — the pursuit and attainment of raw power. It doesn't matter if it's the church, a civic club or booster organization — he must run it. This person can be so unpredictable because he will change his opinions to fit whatever he thinks will give him the power.

Why does criticism hurt so much? Often it is because we suspect they may be right. If not, we live in fear that they will convince others that they are right. Criticism hurts because it goes straight to matters of our essential selves. It often deals with our competence and our personality.

When dealing with a critic try not to take it personally — it is rarely personal. The critic would deal with any minister the way he deals with you. It is so difficult not to take it personally, but every leader must develop a thick skin. Imagine what it must be like for an actor to see the critics' opinions on his performance. Think of what any president of the United States must live with.

One excellent piece of advice is to be careful of the person who initially befriends you. Often he is trying to align you with his agenda. When you show an independent mind, he abandons you, or worse, opposes you.

Don't let the criticism affect your public attitude and performance. Morning worship is God's time. It is time to worship, not time to scold the congregation or to reveal your innermost thoughts.

What do you say to defuse a critic? Often we can simply say things like:

"You may be right."
"Thank you for bringing this to my attention."
"I'm sure sorry; I didn't intend to hurt or offend you."
"I'll surely take that into consideration."

One well-known church leader, if he gets a mean letter, photocopies it and highlights the nastiest parts.

He then mails it back to the critic with a note that says something like, "In the heat of the moment, I often express myself more severely than I intended. In case that happens to you as well, I have returned your letter. If, after reading it, you still feel the same way, mail the letter back and I will respond." He claims he has rarely seen the letter the second time.

We would not necessarily want to use the solution of one Christian leader who boldly wrote to his critic and said, "I think you need to know that some lunatic is writing me using your name." H. L. Mencken, the newspaper man, once wrote to a critic, "I am sitting here with your letter before me. Soon it will be behind me." One prominent Christian leader responded simply and kindly to a severe critic by saying, "I guess I am just destined to be a disappointment to you." While these responses are clever, they will not work any better than the advice of Solomon who told us a soft answer turns away wrath. Every minister must read Marshall Shelly's masterpiece, *Well-Intentioned Dragons*. It has saved many a minister and many a ministry. We must believe his title, no matter how difficult it is. We can believe there are dragons about, but it is hard to see them as well-intentioned. We do well to remember Shelly's observation that often dragons are wounded sheep. The old adage "Hurt people hurt people" is as true as any adage gets.

The Minister and Time Management

Basic to all administration is the ability to manage time. All of us are guilty of poor time management, so much so that procrastination is nearly a universal problem.

It is essential that we manage time. In fact, we all do, either poorly or effectively. If you don't manage your time, someone or something else will. It is nearly axiomatic that success in ministry will be directly related to your ability to manage time. You must believe that you have the power to change your time habits. Admittedly, our temperament will greatly affect our ability and willingness to control time. Still, we can improve. Our goal is not to become a time nut or an excessive clock-watcher. Tools are abundant for those interested in time management. Many of the books share similar approaches with differing nomenclatures. Let's consider some helpful time management strategies, particularly appropriate for the minister.

First, *remember your central purpose and priorities.* This will greatly determine the decisions you make about the specific use of time in a given moment. We do not have total control over this decision. The Scriptures and our employers will certainly be factors to consider.

Learn how to delegate responsibility and authority. So much is written about delegation that we fear for the poor guy who has to do all the work while everyone else sits around and thinks. Some things cannot be delegated, but when you do delegate, give sufficient authority for the person to fulfill the responsibilities. At first delegation takes more time, but down the line, as the person learns to function on his own, it will save time.

Learn how to say, "No." This is very difficult for preachers because we want to please people. If you are offered a speaking engagement or committee assignment you honestly believe you cannot fulfill adequately, it is far better to say no and give them a minor disappointment than to say "Yes," fail, and give them a major disappointment.

Be ready for interruptions. Ministers can never fully avoid interruption for often interruptions are our job. Much of the best and most significant ministry we do, starts as an interruption. This does not mean that you cannot protect some office hours by requiring appointments for counseling sessions.

Learn to consolidate activities. Take a book to the doctor's office. You know you have to wait. Why not study while you wait? Listen to books on tape while you are in the car. Exercise while you watch television.

Most important is the use of a calendar system. There are so many out there, like Day-Timers, Day Runner, Franklin, Filofax and others. Most of them use similar principles. Find a system and use it. It doesn't matter what brand you buy if you don't use it. Some like the larger binder systems. Some like the smaller pocket version. It doesn't matter. Pick one and use it consistently. Take your planner with you wherever you go. Write things down so you won't clutter your mind trying to remember everything. Particularly helpful is a to-do list. You should make one every day, prioritize your list and do them in the order of importance. When you miss an appointment, you know it's because of absent-mindedness, but the offended party will interpret it as not caring.

Don't be afraid to use the wastebasket. Ministers receive a lot of junk mail. File it or trash it. Don't just pile it. Try to handle each piece of paper only once. Respond to it.

Keep the door to your office closed. This does not mean you are not accessible, but it will cut down on visitors who are just passing by and don't want to be so rude as to ignore you.

Learn to close a conversation. That goes for the phone as well as a private conversation. Many of us treat phone calls like infatuated adolescents, not wanting to be the first to hang up. Learn to say, "I've got to go now, is there anything else we need to discuss?" When it comes to an office visit, you can tell the visitor up front, how much time you have. When you sense the conversation has run its course, you can simply stand up, move toward the door and thank the visitor for his input.

Group related activities together. Answer all your mail at one time. Make all your call-backs at one time. Study for sermon and Sunday school lessons can be symbiotic.

Learn to use a computer. This is the great time saver or time waster of our times. It all depends on our discipline. The first few days of computer literacy are frustrating and many wonder if it will be worth it. After mastering the basic techniques it can greatly reduce sermon writing time. Beware of playing games or surfing the Net excessively.

Use the services of a secretary. An organized secretary can make an unorganized preacher look good. Give her work to do even when you are out of town. Let her track down people you are trying to call.

The Minister and Stewardship

Most church boards will tell the minister he is not responsible for the finances. They mean well, but the first person to get blamed when the finances are poorly handled is the minister. Stewardship is really a spiritual matter, so the minister ought to take a personal interest in stewardship education and development.

Most churches have only begun to reach their giving potential. The principal reason is either a lack of education in stewardship or a lack of motivation for stewardship. It has been well said that no church has financial problems. The only kind of problem a church can have is a spiritual problem, and if a church thinks it has a financial problem, it is likely that it has a spiritual problem.

Stewardship must never be viewed as a scheme to raise money, but as a plan to grow people. Its goal is givers, not gifts; tithers, not tithes; people, not money. The basic premise of stewardship is a person's need to give. That is far more important than the church's need to receive. The church's need is great and the opportunities for the church are many, but our need to give is greater. One minister said, "If we struck oil on the church lawn tomorrow, we would still need this campaign. Our people need to give." This idea is basic to an understanding of stewardship. This is the reason that such a program can and must be approached without hesitation, without embarrassment, and without apology. The greatest favor you can do for any Christian is to teach him the joy of stewardship and to show him how he can extend his influence beyond the years of his own life and beyond the boundaries of his own family.

People are motivated to give by a recognized sense of opportunity or need. Of the two, opportunity is more appealing than need, although both must be recognized. No one disputes the fact that many opportunities confront the church. The problem is that they have not been vividly and attractively presented to people who have both the resources and the willingness to give.

In order to motivate people to give we must help them develop a positive feeling about the church; negative feelings inhibit giving quickly and drastically. A successful program NEVER dwells on the negative aspects, but always on the positive side of the church's life. Of course, a clear understanding of the biblical principle of stewardship is essential. People must know to whom they belong. They must have made a commitment of themselves and their whole lives to Jesus Christ. They must recognize the long and dignified history of stewardship in both the Old Testament and New.

For people to give it is necessary that they have confidence in the leadership of the church. There must be created and maintained a climate of trust in both the ministerial leadership and in the nonprofessional leadership of the congregation. The great missing link in stewardship is communication. Principles are not communicated. Opportunities are not communicated. The reasons for trust and confidence are not communicated. This is the principal fault in all congregations and the source of most troubles.

Stewardship education should be approached confidently and joyfully. It should be approached because it is a part of the Christian gospel. Stewardship development should be a yearlong affair with an annual emphasis on stewardship, just as we have special emphases at Christmas or Easter. It will become an accepted fact of the life of the church. But the annual emphasis must be coupled with yearlong attention to stewardship details, encouragement, reports, and accountability.

Good stewardship education does not settle for appeals to pity, pride, social embarrassment, approval of others, tax advantages, conscience-salving, indebtedness to God or the community, or loyalty to the group. It does appeal to love, loyalty to God, opportunities to make one's life count, joyful participation, and joyful partnership in the great work God is doing in our world.

Pledging is a very helpful tool for sound financial planning for any congregation. Without some idea of anticipated income it will be difficult for the church to plan its expenditures intelligently. Some think the word "pledge" sounds harsh. They choose to call it a commitment, faith promise, planned giving, statement of intent. Whatever it is called, the filling out of a card indicating anticipated giving is recommended for stewardship development.

When such a plan is introduced for the first time, resistance is always encountered. It should be met with a smile and with the attitude, "Let's try it. Maybe it won't work, but many churches do it. Let's try it and see." There is such a need for practical help in this area that we have included a step-by-step program for stewardship education in Appendix A.

Your Role in the Community

What is your proper role in community service and community affairs? This is a difficult question to answer. To be completely aloof from such things would certainly be a mistake. Someone has said that community service is the rent you pay for the space you occupy on earth.

Certainly, we have concerns beyond our congregation. On the other hand, such things can take an enormous amount of time and energy. You will find that both are in short supply.

Many preachers belong to some service club: Lions, Rotary, Optimist, Exchange, Ruritan, or others. Usually this involves little more than a weekly luncheon and a few hours each year for some project. They seldom involve you in anything embarrassing. Of course you will opt out of lotteries, selling chances on some prize, or other things that you cannot countenance. You just politely say, "I have to ask you to leave me out of the loop on this one." Nothing more needs to be said.

If your children are in school, you will probably want to support your parent-teacher organization or booster club. Maybe the friends of the library will appeal to you. You could be involved in a youth organization like Boy Scouts, Girl Scouts or a similar organization.

Holding office in these organizations may be a different matter; it is enormously time consuming. You will have to decide if you have enough time and energy for it. Holding offices beyond the local level in such groups is probably unwise.

You will seldom see any direct benefit from participation in such organizations. Occasionally someone will come to your church because they met you in this way, but it is rare. The benefits are more indirect. Such things as good will and being known in the community have considerable value. Think of your participation as a kind of advertising or public relations.

CHAPTER FIVE

THE MINISTER AS A SHEPHERD

We have lost the biblical image of the Shepherd and substituted for it the corporate image of a Chief Executive Office or a Chief Operating Officer. While many ministers prefer not to use the term "pastor," no one can argue that shepherding is always a part of your duties. Shepherding includes counseling the troubled, ministering to the sick, the dying, the bereaved and conducting funeral services.

Counseling

A generation ago counseling was a very minor part of your work. Today it has become a very significant one. You must remember that counseling is very time consuming. It concentrates many hours of work on a very few people. Good stewardship of your time will require that you keep counseling to a minimum. You will need to remember that we are vulnerable here. While anybody can sue anybody else any time they choose, you are not really liable if your counseling is spiritual. If you get into psychological counseling, you can be held liable for malpractice. While your knowledge of psychology will underlie your counseling

81

and inform it, you will be wise not to become an unpaid psychiatrist. You will be wise to recognize your limitations and refer people who need extensive help. It is best not to say, "You need a psychiatrist!" It is best to say, "I am really in over my head on this and I am going to recommend a professional counselor." The word *counselor* is better received than the words *psychologist* or *psychiatrist.* You may want to add, "If you asked me to take out your appendix, I'd have to refuse because I am not competent to do that. We have reached the limit of my competency here."

It is well to think of your counseling largely as first aid. It is good also to remember that most people are not really coming to you for advice. Some of them want you to agree with what they have already decided. You should neither agree nor disagree, unless they're talking about some violent act or some criminal act. In such cases you say flatly, "No! Don't do that!" If they are discussing some sinful act, you can say, "I know that you would not expect me as a Christian minister to say that that is all right." You can ask penetrating questions that will help them see the problem differently or see some aspects of it that they are not now seeing. It is tempting to bring out verses of Scripture that inform the situation but it is usually not very helpful. People in distress are not ready for you to quote Scripture to them.

Most people who will come to you are really looking for someone to listen sympathetically. There is much to be said for nondirective counseling, especially where we ministers are concerned. To show that you're listening, look the person in the eye, don't interrupt or contradict, and occasionally repeat what they have said to show that you are listening. In many cases all they wanted was for someone to listen. In many cases the necessity of verbalizing their feelings so they can express them to you helps them to see things more clearly.

It is essential that you keep the sessions to one hour or less. Beyond that time the conference will not be productive. You signal that when they make an appointment. "I can see you from 2:00 until 3:00 tomorrow afternoon." You signal it again when the time is up by standing. You will usually then pray. If they do not take that hint, begin walking toward the door. Open the door for them. Suggest that they may want call you if they need to talk again.

The things people tell you in counseling are sacred and you must *never* repeat them. Generally, the law provides for this confidentiality even in the courtroom. However, the clergy privilege is not as absolute as it once was. There is often a difference in the eyes of the law concerning what someone tells you as a confession and what someone tells you as part of a counseling session. There are some exceptions depending on state laws. There are also some variations depending on the interpretation of a judge, who may, if he feels there is a compelling state interest, revoke clergy privilege. This is used only in the most extreme cases when child abuse or the threat of possible physical harm is a possibility. It would be wise to check with an attorney concerning the laws in your state.

There is no way to guarantee you won't be sued. We live in a very litigious society. By all means make sure your church has counseling liability as part of its insurance package. Still, in the vast majority of cases, you are not *required* to testify to what a person has said to you as his or her spiritual leader. This is true even if they have confessed a crime to you. In such extreme cases you may choose to testify but you are not required to do so.

Most states now require child abuse to be reported. Some states have CARL provisions. CARL stands for Child Abuse Reporting Law. These laws require religious workers to report child abuse and legally protect the one who reports. If someone else tells you of child abuse, you are required to report it. Other than that, tell no one what has been revealed to you in the counseling session. Do not use it as a sermon illustration — unless you are a guest speaker in a church far away from the one you serve. Even then, it will suggest that you really cannot be trusted with a secret. It may be best to tell it in the third person, "A member once said to his minister. . ."

You will discover that if you do go into extensive counseling and get deeply into a person's mind and heart, they will leave the church you serve. They are not going to sit there every Sunday and listen to a preacher who knows the darkest secrets of their lives. Of course, you are far too busy to remember such things, but they don't know that. Be prepared for that if your counseling delves deeply into the person's inner life.

Sometimes something will come up in counseling that is going to be dealt with in next Sunday's sermon. You must tell them, "By coincidence, I plan to speak of these things in my sermon next Sunday. I don't want you to think that I decided to do that just now. I don't want you to think that that sermon is reflecting what we've just talked about. I planned to preach this sermon weeks ago, and I have already prepared most of it. I just wanted you to know that my sermon is in no way an extension of our conversation today."

As we will discuss in the next chapter, realize that you are most vulnerable to being misunderstood when counseling people about marital difficulties. Keep two pictures of your wife and family in your office, one turned so the counselee can see it and one turned so you can see it. Do not touch the counselee if there is any hint of their becoming attached to you — and if you do give them a reassuring touch, do it on the way out in front of your secretary. Do not meet persons of the opposite sex alone at the church. Someone else must be present in the office area, though not in the counseling room itself. If it is not your secretary, it can be another staff member, your wife, or even a trusted member of the church who can keep quiet the identity of your visitor.

It is comforting to know that it is not your obligation to solve the problems of people who come to you. Some are beyond solving. And the problem is their problem. You must not make it your problem. You can help them to see ways that may move toward solution, but it is generally agreed that you cannot share insights. You cannot say, "I see your problem. It is this." They will not accept your evaluation of the situation. You must try to lead them to be able to say, "I think my problem is. . ." You may ask, "Do you think this would work? What would happen if you tried this?" If you are more directive than that they will not accept it.

Ministering to the Sick

Every preacher should visit in the hospital. Visit your members, visit the relatives of members, and visit those who are friends of the church or prospects for membership in the church. There are several reasons to visit in the hospital. The first is that it is most effective. People need you when they face illness. They need your presence, your prayers, your encouragement. The second is that it is efficient. You can see more of your people in an hour or two in the local hospital than any other time or place. The third is that it is expected. Two thousand years of Christian tradition has led people to expect that the one who stands before them on Sunday morning should stand beside them when they are ill.

When should you visit? The best time is just before visiting hours. The patient will be ready for visitors, but you will not have to share the time with other visitors. As a minister you are permitted to visit the hospital at any time. If you have several hospitals to visit, you cannot fit them all into that time frame. Go at whatever time of day you can. The only exception is in the maternity section. Some hospitals have a policy of only allowing visits during visiting hours. Check with the individual hospital. You might want to have a nurse make sure the patient is ready for a visitor before entering the room.

Most hospitals have a clergy list at the desk. Look under your church, but also look under the classifications "Protestant" and "No Religion Listed." You will often find your members there. If the list is not long, scan the whole list to see if there are names you recognize. Go to the room. If the door is open, walk in asking, "May I come in?" If the door is closed tap on the door, begin to open it slowly and ask, "May I come in?" If it is an embarrassing time, this gives the patient the opportunity to head you off at the door. Strangely, a patient will sometimes tell you to come in and it will be immediately obvious to you that they should have asked you to wait. Back out saying, "I'll come back in a few minutes." But often the door is closed for some reason that has nothing to do with privacy and you cannot stand all day in front of a hospital door. If doctors or nurses are working with the patient, go back out into the hall and wait for them to leave.

When you enter the room, go directly to the patient. Take their hand unless there is a valid reason not to do so. Ask them how they are. Then speak to others in the room. Speak to the patient who shares the room. Ask general questions about pain, appetite, food. If there are flowers remark on their beauty. Never ask a lady what is wrong with her. In these days of frankness most patients, male or female, will tell you. But it is important to be sensitive to the fact that some female patients do not want to discuss their problem with you. Do not contradict the reported advice of the doctor. It is unethical for you to disagree with their physician. In extreme cases you may want to say, "Have you thought about getting an opinion from another doctor?"

Don't sit down unless the patient indicates a need for a deep discussion of family, of their own death, or for confession. Most will ask you to sit down, but that is not

The Minister as a Shepherd

such an indication, and need not be taken seriously. You say, "Thanks, but I prefer to stand." Don't sit down on the bed, nor in the chair that is indicated or offered. A long visit is generally not in the best interests of the patient. Fifteen minutes would be a long visit. Most will take only five minutes. Almost always you will close with a prayer. There are two exceptions. Sometimes there is such confusion in the room (procedures, loud television, chattering visitors) that prayer would be inappropriate. The other exception is in cases where there has been a long hospitalization, you have visited often and prayed and now the patient is improving and will soon go home. Your omitting prayer on that visit will encourage the patient that you, too, think he or she is well on the road to recovery. But even then, a prayer of thanksgiving is not out of order.

When you pray, it is important to neither raise false hopes nor to suggest pessimistic outcomes. Certainly it is often appropriate to pray for healing. But there are cases where death appears to be inevitable and imminent. Then you pray for strength, for God's presence, without telling God what you think the outcome is going to be and without telling God that he must heal this person. After all, there are cases where death is the ultimate healing. The prayer should be short. While a few ministers read Scripture to the patient, most do not, and it can usually be omitted.

How often should you visit? If you do not choose your practice in advance, you may be accused of favoritism — and it *is* tempting to visit some more than others. Ordinarily, a visit to a patient in a local hospital should be made every other day. If you have a staff, you go on Mondays. More people are in the hospital on Monday than any other day of the week and that will maximize your involvement with your members. Have another staff member go on Wednesday and another on Friday. If you *are* the staff, then you go on Monday, Wednesday and Friday to visit patients in *local* hospitals.

If the patient is in a distant hospital, once a week may be all you can do.

But if the patient is critically ill, go every day. So if you have one critically ill in a certain hospital and you go every day, you will not omit the others who are in the same hospital. Some will thus be seen every day who are not critical — but you cannot be in the building and pass them by. If later you are criticized for visiting some more than others, you can easily explain your practice.

In critical care units you walk in and go directly to the nurses station *first*. Identify yourself and tell them whom you wish to see. They will tell you if there is a procedure going on and then you will be asked to wait. Do so politely. Generally, they will indicate that you may visit at once. Keep the visit short. Do pray. Remember that the last sense we lose is the sense of hearing. A patient may seem comatose and yet be able to hear what you are saying. Do not discuss the condition of the patient with family or others in the presence of the patient.

Once in a while you will have a patient in an isolation room. There will be a sign on the door. Go to the nurses station and identify yourself. They will give you a robe and mask and sometimes something to cover your shoes. Follow their instructions. Make the call brief. Do not touch the patient.

Occasionally the family will be told that a patient is terminally ill and they will decide not to tell the patient. They will ask you not to tell the patient. What should you do? You must respect their wishes, though you may say, "If it were me I'd want to know, but I leave that up to you." What then, if the patient asks you for the prognosis? One minister handled that perfectly. The lady asked, "Am I going to get well?" The minister said, "Now you know me, and you know that I am not a doctor." That was the perfect answer.

Patients facing surgery should be visited before the operation. If the patient is already in the hospital, you can phone the nurses station for that room after 4:00 p.m. the previous evening and they will tell you when your patient is on the surgery schedule. You must arrive two hours prior to that time! They often leave the room an hour ahead of time for preparation. Sometimes schedules are changed and the person moves up on the schedule. No call is more appreciated than the call before surgery.

But often now patients are admitted on the same day as surgery. That means they will be busy from the moment they enter the hospital. The best you can do on those occasions is to visit them in the home the night before, or if you have an appointment, then in the late afternoon of the day before. If all else fails, phone them and pray with them over the telephone! But that is not ideal.

Hospital personnel are very cooperative with ministers who come to pray with patients before surgery. We have often prayed with patients in the hall as they were about to be transported from the room and nurses have often interrupted their work for a minute or two to allow a short prayer, but always ask if you may offer a short prayer. And it should be short. Thank God for the marvels of modern medicine and surgery. Thank God that such operations are possible. Thank God for medicines that relieve pain. Ask that this operation will prove to be just what was needed. Ask Him to bless the doctors and nurses.

It is not good use of your time to wait with the family during surgery unless you are specifically asked to do so. But do ask them to phone you as soon as they learn something. Tell them where you can be reached. Tell them if you are not there, to leave a message. This shows your ongoing concern.

If a patient leaves the hospital for a convalescent facility, visit once a week. If they leave the hospital to go home, make one home visit after they have returned home.

Some people are chronically ill. Visit such patients once a month.

Always remember that Jesus commended those who had visited him when he was sick. They protested that they had never seen him sick. Then he said, "Whatever you did for one of the least of these...you did for me."

Ministering to the Dying

A minister entered a hospital room one day where the patient was terminally ill. She knew that she was dying. She already had a visitor. The patient was crying and the visitor was saying, "Now, now. Don't cry. Everything's going to be all right. God is going to make everything all right." With that the visitor left. The minister pulled a chair up beside the bed, took the patient's hand and sat there in silence. He said nothing. After about ten minutes, the patient said, "You're such a comfort to me." He had not said one word!

What is instructive in that little scene from real life? He did not minimize the patient's grief. He did not tell her not to cry. She had every reason to cry and every right to cry. He did not lie to her. She was not going to get well, and she knew it. He comforted her by his presence, and by his acceptance of the gravity of her situation. We do not help people when we minimize their situation.

Sometimes someone will want to talk with you about her own impending death. Usually she cannot do this with family members. Families will not let people talk about it, and many need to talk about it. So they will want to talk with you. Let them. Don't deny the imminence of their death. Don't deny the awfulness of impending separation from loved ones. Just listen and let them talk. There are some people who handle their impending death by *not* talking about it and that is their privilege. But many people want to talk about it and need to talk about it. If that is the case, they will initiate the conversation. Your job is to listen. That's hard to do. You will never do a harder day's work than when you listen to a person discuss his or her own impending death. Don't tell them that if they only confess their sins, they'll be healed. Don't refuse to believe that they are dying. Often they will want to plan their own funeral. It is a way of remaining in control. Listen. Take notes if you need to jot down funeral details. When they have finished, ask if you may pray. Thank God for the person's courage and faith. Thank God for His everlasting arms. Thank God that Jesus is with us always. Ask God to bless the family.

People who are dying experience the same stages of grief as the bereaved: anger, denial, guilt, bargaining and acceptance. Your only responsibility is to be available. You are not responsible for succeeding in leading them to face death calmly. Most of them will do that, but your only responsibility is to be there, to listen, and to care. You will want to visit more often as death approaches, moving from every other day to every day as you sense the end coming. The conversation they initiate with you when they speak frankly of death and of their concerns will probably only occur once.

Ministering to the Bereaved

When you learn that someone connected with the congregation or one of its families has died, go at once. Drop everything and go! As you go, you will be wondering, "What shall I say?" The answer is, say very little. It is your presence that counts. Go directly to the one closest to the deceased — or to the one you know best — and say, "This is terrible." Put your arm around them. The ministry of touch and the ministry of presence are the things that count here. Don't say things like:

She's in a better place.
It's God's will.
His suffering is over.
She's better off.
I know how you feel.

91

God needed a flower for His Garden.

She's with Jesus now.

They may say some of these things. They have a right to say them. You don't. A lady died who was in her mid-eighties and had been ill for a long time. The daughter said to her minister: "People keep telling me not to be sad: that Mother is better off. But then she was not *their* Mother."

Funeral customs vary from community to community. When you are new in town, go to the local funeral director and ask him if there are any customs that are peculiar to your area. Also talk with a local minister who knows the culture.

If the family wants another minister to conduct the service, be very gracious and tell them that is perfectly all right. But be sure that you attend that funeral! If another minister is in charge and you're assisting, he will suggest what part of the service you are to handle. If you are in charge and there is an assisting minister, you should ask him to read Scripture and pray. If there are three, ask one to do the committal at the grave.

When you are called, be sure you know when the service is, where it will held, where the interment will be and the family names. Be sure you know the hours of visitation. Go to the funeral home at the time of visitation. Go directly to the one closest to the deceased. Put your arm around him or her. Usually the casket will be open and they will want to view the body with you. It is not necessary to say any "comforting words." You need not stay through the whole time of visitation. Ten minutes is long enough. Greet other family members. Meet those family members you don't know. Permit the relatives to talk about the deceased if they wish.

While many ministers ask the family if they want something special for the funeral service, we don't recommend it. Unless they come to you with a special request, conduct the service in the way you normally do. Sometimes the family will give you a poem to read at the funeral that seems to you inappropriate. Read it anyway, but first say the family has asked you to read this because it is especially meaningful to them. If there is music, you can have one song at the beginning and one at the end. If there are three, put the one in the middle. Many ministers have strong feelings about an open casket, but the funeral is not a time to impose your ideas of propriety on grieving people. Let them do whatever they wish in that regard.

Arrive about twenty minutes early for the funeral service. It will probably be in a funeral home, but it may be in your church. If it is to be in your church, be sure you know if they are expecting you to furnish an organist or soloist. Tell the funeral director how you will conclude your service. In most places the service lasts about fifteen minutes. But there are places where that would seem much too short. Know your community customs.

Usually your part of the service will be Scripture, prayer, remarks and a closing prayer. Obituaries used to be common, but they are seldom used now. If there is no obituary, be sure to mention at some point the name of the deceased. An anonymous funeral seems cold. You may begin by saying, "We are here to pay our respects to _____" Or you may put the name in your prayer thanking God for the life of _____ and for the comforting memories his family cherishes.

The funeral sermon is not an opportunity for evangelism. It is unfair to take advantage of a captive audience. It may be an opportunity for pre-evangelism. In your remarks you may want to say some good things about the deceased if he or she was an outstanding person in the church or the community. But the burden of your remarks should be about God and His comfort.

While most funeral services will be restrained, you will occasionally find yourself in a highly charged emotional situation. The one person who must maintain composure is you, even if the persons involved are very close to you. It is your job to remain composed. You may need at some point to force yourself to think of something else in order to do that (such as, "What errand must I attend to when this is finished?").

You will sometimes hold funerals for strangers and sometimes for people who had no church connection and apparently no faith. What do you say? You don't say anything about the deceased except: "I am sure the family today is comforted by many good memories, but our greatest comfort always comes from contemplating God and His mercy." Then talk about God's care for *them*, the relatives and friends. Tell them God wants to come to them in a special way today. That he wants to share their sorrow, as he wants to share our joys.

Do not begin the service of an unbeliever with a disclaimer: "He's in the hands of a just God." This implies that in your view he doesn't have a chance at heaven! Say nothing about the character or lack of character of the deceased. The family knows this already. Tell them about God.

Often you will conduct a service for a stranger. If you are sympathetic, kind and comforting, the family will be in your services the following Sunday. That means you have done a good job of pre-evangelism. They see you as a caring person. You can then build on that first visit to encourage them to return and you can lead the family to Christ.

After you close your funeral service with prayer the funeral director will take over. It may be that there will be a procession as people pass by the casket for a final view. If so, stand at the foot of the casket, but back just a little. You don't want it to look as if you are waiting for compliments on your message — but you do want to stand like an honor guard. Last, the family will view and then you walk up as if you were a member of the family and view the body with them. If there is a delay in leaving the casket, you can put your arm around the clinging mourner and say, "Let's go to the car now." After this it is up to the funeral director to get them away from the casket and into the car.

If there is no post-funeral viewing, then you accompany the casket as it is wheeled out of the church or funeral home.

The custom is that after your service you stay with the casket until it is put into the hearse for the drive to the cemetery. You walk slowly in front of it. Usually you will ride with the funeral director in the lead car. Sometimes you will drive your own. Try not to be the lead car. You may not know where the grave is.

At the cemetery park your car and go immediately to the hearse. You will then walk ahead of the casket to the gravesite. Then step aside so the casket can be placed on the lowering device. The funeral director will usually tell you which is the head of the casket. You stand at the head. When the group assembles, the funeral director will nod to you. That is your signal to begin the committal. This is not another sermon. It may be a few words of Scripture and a prayer. It may be a sentence like this: "Our hearts still cling to the body, because we cannot disassociate ourselves from the loved one who dwelt in it and animated it. Yet we know that the body is only the earthly dwelling place, the house of clay, the tenement of time now vacated for that larger house not made with hands, eternal in the Heavens. So we are certain that the true individual is not here, but already in the presence of God. Therein lies our comfort and our hope." Then offer a brief prayer. (Notice that the above committal is carefully worded. It doesn't say the deceased is in heaven, but in the *presence* of God. Even a condemned sinner will be in the *presence* of God for judgment if not for reward. This is a carefully worded committal and a safe thing to say in any circumstance.

After you have finished your final prayer say, "This concludes the service." People will still just stand there. So you go along the front row of the mourners and shake hands with each one. What shall you say? All you need to say is, "God bless you." When you finish, the people will finally begin to sense that it is over and to mingle. You, too, mingle with the crowd if there are those there you know — and then get in your car and leave.

You will face difficult funerals: suicide, murder, the death of a child. It is well always to speak of God and His comfort, of Christ and His love and not to try to explain things that we cannot explain. You can say, "We do not know how to understand what has happened. I would be less than honest with you if I tried to explain. There is much we do not know. But I want to talk of something we do know. We know that we are not alone in our grief. We know that our Lord shares our sorrows."

Many times the family will have a meal somewhere after the funeral and invite you. Unless the meal is being served in your church, or in the home of a member of your church, you may want to excuse yourself saying, "I have another base I have to touch." You need not be specific about what that base is. Nothing is so awkward as being with a mourning family you do not even know trying to eat and make conversation. About a week after the funeral visit the home. Then in three or four weeks make a second visit. You need to show an ongoing concern after the funeral.

Sometimes you will have to deliver a death message. This is most difficult. There is no easy way to break the news, but there is a gradual way. The conversation goes like this:

They: Well, how are you today.

You: Not very good, I have some bad news.

They: What is it?

You: John's been in an accident.

They: Was he badly hurt?

You: Yes, he was.

They: Is he going to be o.k.?

You: No.

They: Is he alive?

You: No.

This will be followed by an explosion of grief. Allow the person to cry, scream, wring their hands, or whatever. You need say no more for a few minutes. Your presence is enough. Then they will begin to ask for details. Give them as much as you can. Don't tell them that he is with Jesus or some other non-comforting words. Then ask if there are family or friends you can call. They will need someone to be with them. You do not want to leave them until someone else comes. You or they make some phone calls. When others arrive you can then offer prayer and leave, telling them to call you if they need anything. Sometime later that day or the next day you can visit again.

CHAPTER SIX

THE MINISTER AND MARRIAGE

While being asked to perform a wedding is a great privilege, it is often among a minister's least favorite activities. It is time intensive, with counseling sessions, rehearsals, dinners and receptions. It is filled with complicated details, which must be addressed while people are stressed-out and nervous. Nevertheless, every minister desires to do a wedding with effectiveness and dignity. What do you need to do to be ready?

Preliminaries

First, you need an ordination. This is not true in every case. Requirements vary from state to state. Generally, a minister, to be qualified to perform weddings, needs an ordination certificate, license to preach, or a resolution from a local church authorizing the minister to perform those duties.

In addition, in some states you must register. Some states have no registration procedure at all. Others require you to register with a state office like the Secretary of State, while still others require you to register with the county clerk. You must check the laws where you live to discover the process in your area.

Failure to do so can result in a most embarrassing circumstance, if you try to perform a wedding without being legally authorized to do so.

Next, you need a service book. There are several on the market that give you a choice of wedding ceremonies. Most couples will have no problem with one of the services in the book. Many ministers choose the service from the Anglican *Book of Common Prayer* or a service that is quite similar to it. In the previous decades the trend had been for couples to write their own vows or do something avant-garde. The new trend is to go back to the traditional. Most want the traditional service and formality is making a comeback. This is a curious phenomenon considering that everything else in society is moving toward informality. Still, from time to time you will have to make judgments on something the couple wants added to the service.

Every minister should have a record book in which he records his weddings, along with baptisms and funerals. Among other reasons to do this is for your own satisfaction. A quick review of the lives you have touched might be a real spirit lifter.

Don't forget you need to purchase appropriate clothing. In some traditions this decision is easily solved by the wearing of a clerical robe. The majority of you will probably not use one. What should you wear? The principle is to not call attention to yourself at all. Some ministers purchase a simple tuxedo. More often a simple black or charcoal gray suit with a white shirt and a dark tie will suffice.

Just having the right credentials is not all that is required of a minister. You must have a personal wedding policy. In some cases, the congregation you serve will establish that policy. It is often true that the minister has a great deal of influence over that policy.

Perhaps the greatest problem a minister faces is how to handle the divorce issue. Some ministers simply refuse to do any second marriages. If you choose this route, you must be prepared to live with your policy even if the chairman of the elders asks you to do the ceremony for his divorced daughter or son. You must be prepared to stick with your policy even if your own sister or daughter asks for an exception.

The Bible does not prohibit all divorce, but it does regulate it. Many ministers will perform a ceremony for an innocent party in a divorce. In one sense there is no one totally innocent in any divorce, but there is the one who broke the covenant and the one who did not. The Bible certainly appears to allow divorce without sin for the innocent party in a marriage where the other spouse was guilty of unfaithfulness or desertion. The problem for a preacher who tries to examine causes of a divorce is that he is easily deceived. Of course that is an ethical problem for the liar, not the preacher.

Some reason that even in an illegitimate divorce there is the possibility of remarriage, if there has been repentance and restoration. One thing we should say for certain is that regardless of your marriage policy, divorce should not be treated as the unforgivable sin. No one denies that fornication in youth can be forgiven. No one denies adultery can be forgiven. Why then do so many feel that divorce cannot be forgiven?

It is always problematic when a person from the community comes to ask you to do a wedding. Often, they have no intention of ever becoming a part of your church community. They are just looking for a church building and someone to sign the papers. Some ministers structure their response in such ways as to encourage the couple to come to church. Others simply refuse to do such weddings. Minimally, if the minister performs the wedding, the fee structure ought to reflect the fact that these people have not been supporting the church financially. In such cases there should be no discomfort in charging a sensible fee. (Some ministers turn this into an evangelistic tool, by waiving their fee if the couple will attend the church at least three consecutive Sundays. There is no hard evidence of how effective this is.)

Another difficult issue arises when a minister is asked to marry a Christian to a nonbeliever. This would seem contrary to the biblical admonition to not unequally yoke a believer with an unbeliever. In spite of this, many who choose to marry in this circumstance will think the minister unkind if he declines to marry them under these conditions. When it comes to the matter of being involved with an unequal yoking, the modern minister has a problem. Just because a person is of a different fellowship, does that make him or her an unbeliever? We must remember that when the Scripture gave us this admonition, there were not the hundreds of denominations we have today. There is no easy answer for this. Some couples will find a church group they can come together in. How dissimilar do church backgrounds have to be before they become problematic?

Another significant problem for the minister is when he is asked to perform a marriage ceremony for a couple who have already begun living together. Television and movies have shown living together as a norm and even some Christian couples have chosen this arrangement. The church needs to be clear on this subject. Living together is frequently institutionalized fornication. Countless studies and anecdotal evidence prove that those who live together without the benefit of clergy have less of a success rate than those who do not live together prior to the marriage. Marriage is not something that can be practiced. The one missing element in living together is the most crucial — commitment. This does not make the church's problem any easier. On the one hand, we do not want to appear to be endorsing living together before marriage. On the other hand, we do not want them to continue to live in this condition, so denying them a wedding makes us deny them the very thing they ought to do.

There are several ways ministers and churches have tried to handle this. The most strict is to simply refuse to do the wedding. In this case, the minister refers them to a justice of the peace. In other cases, a church might allow the minister to do a small, private wedding, but not a full church wedding. The idea is to help them to do the right thing, but to make a statement about the church's insistence on marriage. Some churches have required the couple to live apart before the wedding if they want a church ceremony. Be prepared for people to resist this. They may try to find another minister and another church. One clever idea some ministers have tried is to require the couple to have a small, private legal ceremony immediately and then they can have the church ceremony with all the trappings later. This idea has a lot of potential.

We have never had any couple say, "Well, if you won't marry us then it must be wrong, so we won't get married at all." They will get married whether you do the ceremony or not. You may want to consider the value of an ongoing ministry to this couple if you marry them, versus losing them to another church if you refuse.

Special problems arise when ministers are asked to perform a ceremony for a pregnant bride. Some of the same issues come into play here as come into play in our discussion concerning living together. If the couple was already engaged and anticipated the wedding night, the wedding might be performed without great concern. After all, they would not be the only sexually active couple ever in a church wedding. They just have more evidence of the sin. The most difficult challenge is when the couple is quite young. It makes little sense to compound the sin by joining together two people who have no business getting married. They may not even be mature enough to make such a commitment. Obviously, we would not counsel for abortion, but we might counsel for adoption. Be prepared for many objections. Young people often think it would be "cute" to have a baby. Parents of the couple often feel adoption is an avoidance of responsibility. If adoption is ruled out and the girl has strong family support, then she might be able to meet the challenge as a single mother. With family support, even some very young couples have faced their responsibility and formed a fine marriage, proving the value of integrity and the power of the grace of God. Often in such cases, a small, private wedding is in order.

There are other issues that may need to be discussed with a couple. These are issues that would not preclude their marriage, but would present enough hardship that they would need to discuss the unique challenges of their situation and to be prepared to deal with it. Issues like this might include a wide age difference or cultural differences.

Premarriage Counseling

Most ministers will be expected to offer some kind of pre-marriage counseling. Most ministers want to do this. We don't want to be "marryin' Sam." We must help the couple see that they can get married in a few minutes, but it will take a lifetime to understand all the ramifications of being married. How many sessions should you have? Ideally, if you had nothing else to do a half-dozen would not be too many. Ministers have so many other responsibilities and the couple is not really prepared to listen, so three is probably more realistic. Some ministers get by with one or two. In large churches they may turn over the premarriage counseling to a specialist on the staff, but most often it is the responsibility of the one performing the ceremony.

What should you talk about? Consider this little five point outline for your first session. It covers the basic areas of conflict in marriage. These are the problems couples talk about in post-marriage counseling.

104

First, talk about money. You can share with them some basic instruction in money management and budgeting. You can talk to them about the dangers of debt.

Secondly, talk about sex. This is a difficult subject for many reasons. Sometimes the couple has already been sexually active and are afraid to admit it. Some couples are shy about discussing the issue at all. Even some ministers are shy about talking about it. There is also the danger that the minister will talk frankly about it for some prurient interest in learning about people's private lives. Assure the couple that they can ask you anything and tell them to share to their own level of comfort. The minister may choose to recommend books for them to read. The minister may also suggest a visit to the physician to discuss the technical aspects. Still, some basic information about the sexual side of marriage from a Christian perspective must be discussed.

Then, you should talk about children. Some couples have never discussed how many they want and when they will start. Some discussion of birth control may be appropriate here. Much of that can be handled by a physician. A new problem that could be discussed is the increase in cases of infertility. Couples need to be reminded that they are a family when they get married and that marriage is not just for the biological production of children. If a couple goes through infertility problems, it will be one of the greatest trials of their lives. Some marriages do not survive it. We will say more about this later.

You should also discuss relationships with in-laws. Fortunately most of the jokes about in-laws are only jokes. Still, there are occasions where parents are against the wedding. Even in the best of situations, great in-laws can unintentionally interfere. The couple should discuss their feelings about this and their strategies for coping.

Finally, you should talk about communication. This is a catchall for the other issues. Couples need to be reminded that even as they share years together, they never outgrow the need to talk out problems. Couples should not be endlessly analyzing their relationship, but neither should they assume their spouse should "just know."

In a second session you might deal with the biblical teachings on marriage. Of course you will want to stress that the Bible teaches that marriage is meant to be for a lifetime. A minister should never change the vows of "as long as we both shall live" to "as long as we both shall love." While human beings are weak and sometimes do not live up to their promises, there is little hope for a marriage if they fail to make a biblical covenant. If you perform a marriage for divorced people, you can say to them something like, "While you can't unscramble the egg, you can determine from this day forth to live in marriage as God has called you."

In the third session you might spend the bulk of the time on the logistics of the wedding itself. You will probably have been talking about some of the arrangements all along, but this will be a good time to finalize the plans. It is good to give them a copy of the church's wedding policies. Maybe you can assist them with a checklist of things to do before a wedding (see appendix).

The Rehearsal and Ceremony

Many ministers report hating the rehearsal. It can be frustrating. Many participants show up late. Some do not show at all. The rehearsal usually takes place the night before the wedding. If all cooperate it should be finished in no more than an hour. Couples can be encouraged to select a wedding coordinator, a friend or relative, who can handle details and settle disputes. Some larger churches provide such a service. If there is no one filling that position, then the minister often has to serve in that capacity at the rehearsal.

At the rehearsal, you will want to take the wedding party through the routine twice. You may or may not want to go through every word of the ceremony. You do need to go through all the actions that the wedding party will need to perform. That involves ushers, lighting candles, exchanging rings, etc. Urge them not to be obsessed with making small mistakes. Assure them that there are very few mistakes even noticed by the audience and what mistakes do happen are forgotten by the reception. At the close of the rehearsal remind them to come early for the wedding and to allow for more time than they think they need. It is also good to pray with the wedding party.

Be early enough for the ceremony to handle the small problems that arise. Give the service the dignity it deserves. After the service, a wise photographer will get your picture right away so you can get to other duties. Don't be surprised, or offended if the photographer forgets you. It is your duty to get the necessary signatures on the document. Usually you will have the best man and maid of honor to sign as witnesses. It is then your responsibility to get the license in the mail. Why not drop it in the post office mailbox on your way out of the church?

You don't have to stay for the entire reception. If you do not know the couple well, they may not miss you at all. Perhaps you can drop in and make a few greetings and leave early so you may attend to other duties.

What about accepting money for your services? An honorarium is customary. If someone asks what you charge for a wedding, you simply say that you have no specific fee, but an honorarium is customary. You might want to charge a fee for nonmembers. Don't be surprised if they forget to pay you. Some day you will receive much more for a wedding than you deserve and it will all balance out.

107

Post-Marriage Counseling

You will be consulted by couples who have run into difficulties in their marriage. You will find this specialized kind of counseling difficult. Ask a lot of questions. You may even have to bring up the matter of sexuality, but be sure you do not ask such questions for any unholy or impure reason.

Nondirective counseling will serve you well in marriage counseling. Suppose you tell a wife she must not leave her husband and he later kills her? This could happen. You don't have to live with that other person, so you should hesitate to tell them to do so.

Your role is to be a sympathetic listener; one who does not appear to take sides. Your role is to help them see aspects of the situation that they may not see. Often, they are focusing on specific events and overlooking others. Your questions may help them see the picture more clearly.

Your questions may help them to consider the future difficulties they now overlook in a rush to end the marriage. If you ask politely about the children, money, home and other practical questions you may cause them to pause and consider.

Scripture should be used, but sparingly. It may be useful to ask them to read I Corinthians 13 when they get home. You may suggest some passages from Proverbs that will help them shed light on their situation. In most cases they do not have to be shown the passages that show the wrongness of what they are considering. If they have been in church, they know that. In our secular society there may be some misunderstandings about what the Bible teaches. You may simply ask them if they have considered what those passages teach. Coming across like an ancient prophet will do little to change their minds, but it will certainly compound the guilt. As in all counseling sessions, keep it to one hour. Offer a prayer for them at the end. Tell them you will be their minister no matter what they decide to do, but always work with them to save the marriage. You need not tell them that from experience you know some marriages are doomed to fail and sometimes divorce is inevitable. It will comfort you to know that, but it will not help them to know that. Recommend good books, resources or seminars that might help them.

If a divorce does occur, one or both may leave your church out of embarrassment. Usually one will stay. You must convey that you love and accept them even though you would have liked to see the marriage succeed. All divorced persons feel some guilt — even innocent parties. All feel a sense of failure. They do not need to be rejected by the church. Because a person has a failed marriage does not mean that they do not love the Lord or do not take the Bible seriously. Assure such persons that you are still their minister, and will help in any way you can. Do not demand they give up everything dear to them in the church. It will do no harm for that person to continue to sing in the choir, be an usher, greeter or treasurer of his or her Sunday School class. Of course if they hold a very public office, if the person is an elder or teacher, something should be done. Often they will do this themselves, but not always. It is best to handle it quietly, informally and with great kindness. This means you may need to do the job. It is best to say, "I think you should sit on the sidelines for a while until the dust settles." This is far better than firing them. While it is a kind of resignation on their part, you did not use the word "resign" when you suggested they "sit on the sidelines."

Remember that a divorced wife feels enormously rejected and is therefore very vulnerable. You must be careful she does not transfer affection to you. If there is any hint of that you must say, "I want to be your minister. I do not want to be anything else. I cannot be anything else but that — your minister."

Divorce is so prevalent, any church mid-sized or

above should have a ministry to the divorced. It is best handled by a support group of people who have gone through the same thing. Obviously, you don't want this to become a dating service. On the other hand people with similar life experience can help when others cannot.

Dealing With Infertility

Here is an area of concern that is seldom recognized. It is the need to minister comfort to couples who are childless. For multiple reasons no one is quite sure about, infertility is on the rise. While some couples are childless by choice, many are not, and it is a great burden to them. Never make jokes about this. Never tease them about it. Recognize that their grief is comparable to the grief of a couple who has lost a child in death. To them it is the death of their dream. In their minds the unborn child already existed. Now they know that that child will never be. Infertile couples go through a genuine grieving process. It is often a great strain on the marriage.

Celebrate the adoption of a child into church families the same way you would any birth. It may give others an idea. Adoption is a long and costly process. Couples may have already tried every medical process known to science. They may have prayed diligently for divine intervention. They need support and encouragement.

Couples who do not have children sometimes mistakenly assume that God has denied them that privilege. When we have opportunity, we need to absolve God from responsibility for this. Couples frequently feel a sense of guilt, as if God thought they were unworthy to be parents or He was punishing them for some past offense. As you have opportunity to share, try to show them that many children are born to parents far less responsible than they are. This is a physical problem and should be treated as other medical problems. Encourage adoption. If they are comfortable with it, give them opportunities for child care or teaching in the church. This sometimes helps them satisfy the need to be maternal or paternal. Above all, never tell them that they should just relax and think positive. Never tell them to just trust and pray harder. They have done all of this and more.

CHAPTER SEVEN

THE MINISTER AND OTHER MINISTERS

No minister works in total isolation. He is part of a great profession and has to consider his obligations to colleagues.

No more awkward relationship exists than that of a minister and his successor or predecessor. He is a brother yet a competitor. If his ministry was positive, he may be seen as a threat to one's self-image. If his ministry was negative, then his influence can have a negative impact for years. Even the most sincere can find these relationships difficult if not impossible. In the interest of church unity as well as ministerial ethics, it is good to consider the proper behavior that should be displayed toward these two colleagues. Since there is no external, objective standard of proper behavior, this discussion will depend on biblical principle, experience and common sense.

How to Treat a Successor

An old adage says, "I want my successor to do well, but not too well." To a certain extent the new minister is responsible for the tone and direction of his own ministry, but the departing minister should do nothing

113

to hinder him. How can a minister help his successor?

First, he can pass on helpful information, but not gossip. The new minister needs to know something of congregational traditions and culture. The former minister must resist telling him information that might spoil his relationship with the people. A new start might be just what some people need. He should only be warned about the most dangerous people in the church. You might give the new minister a report on the general state of the church, reminders about church traditions and upcoming programming.

It is also important that the departing minister never criticize the new minister in the presence of a church member. In the secret places of his own heart, the former minister may agree with the criticisms he hears. He may even feel a certain vindication of his own ministry. Still, the church cannot grow healthily under those conditions. Any criticisms you feel are essential, and very few if any are, must be delivered directly to the new minister in private. This way he will know that his predecessor has everyone's best interests at heart. Before you dare to criticize, remember how it affects you. You may choose to remain silent. This is best in the vast majority of cases. Church members may criticize the new minister in your presence. You can communicate by your silence and general demeanor that you will not participate. Defend him if possible. Praise him if appropriate. Sure, you might do things differently, but that doesn't make it an issue of right and wrong.

Those who supported your ministry may think that criticizing a successor is a kind of tribute to their former leader. The former minister must stay out of these church quarrels. He may even have to ask his supporters to treat the new man kindly as a personal favor.

Next, the former minister should resist coming back for weddings and funerals. How is the new minister ever going to develop a pastoral relationship with the people, if he is not allowed to share in the significant moments of their lives? Some weddings and funerals may be inevitable, but if they are accepted, the former minister should consult with and brief his successor.

Another warning should be issued to retiring ministers or those changing vocations. They should not stay at the church where they used to minister. If they do return, it should be after the successor has had sufficient time to establish his own ministry. This may be difficult, but in most cases, it is the wisest course of action. However sentimental a minister feels, he must realize that the church he is leaving is no longer his flock; he may love the people, but he is not their shepherd. To leave means to leave. You can't be constantly getting involved as if you were still the minister. Pack up your opinions with your belongings. Have a wonderful emotional and tearful farewell, but don't look back.

How to Treat a Predecessor

Anecdotal evidence would suggest that most of the problems come from predecessors. This makes sense from a sociological and psychological perspective. Still there are times when a successor can cause trouble. In addition, there are things a successor can do to make the transition more pleasant. First, a successor should not be jealous of the congregation's love for the former preacher. W.A. Criswell used to say, "Do not be jealous of your predecessor. Embalm him in honey, not in vinegar." The people will love and admire you for it. In most cases, those who love their departing preacher will eventually transfer that love to the new man. The congregation is going through a kind of grief over the loss of a preacher. It is important to let them continue to love him. As hard as it may be, a new minister should not be troubled by the affection a church has for a former minister. They probably didn't love him that much when he was there. A few may praise the former minister to be irritating, but most do it innocently. It is best to ignore it and go on with your ministry.

In those cases where the former minister was not popular or had committed some kind of moral indiscretion, it is probably best not to discuss him at all. The church needs to put the event behind them. They probably did their grieving before the new minister arrived; it's time for a new and positive tone.

Secondly, the new minister should not try to blame the former minister for the problems he sees in the church. He should remember that the previous minister probably struggled to solve these problems. If the new preacher's ministry is difficult, the only target he has is the old preacher. Just as the old minister should not criticize the successor, so the new minister should not criticize his predecessor. Every minister leaves behind some enemies too. Those who did not like the old minister may befriend the new preacher at first. But if he disappoints them, they may just as easily turn on the new man. Remember, the longer you are there, the less you will hear either criticism or praise. Eventually it will stop.

Finally, the new minister should be gracious about weddings, funerals and the like. If the predecessor has had a long ministry, it is only natural that people would request him for weddings and funerals. If he does accept these dates, it may simply be because of soft-heartedness, not because of malice toward the new man. At any rate the families should not be penalized for their sentimentality. There may even come a time when the minister might invite the old preacher back for a special service, anniversary or homecoming. This should only happen when the new preacher is fully accepted into the leadership and pastoral roles.

With God's help, even the most awkward of relationships can be reconciled. It will never be easy; no man can make the right decisions all the time. Still, with determination and spiritual sensitivity a minister can pass on his flock to another shepherd with dignity and grace. This is surely the way God wants it done. One minister left a note to his successor. This is what it said, "I was not as good as my friends will tell you I was. I am not as bad as my enemies will tell you I was. I believe if you love these people, they will love and accept you." That's a classy way to leave.

How to Treat a Colleague

It is rare for a lawyer to publicly criticize another lawyer. Rarer still do you see a physician criticize another physician. Ministers are one of the few professionals who openly criticize each other. This ought not to be. It often happens when one minister achieves some degree of success or renown, others find some reason to declare him arrogant, unfriendly or hypocritical. Often these offenses are only in the mind of the criticizer. Maybe it helps him deal with his own relative lack of success. It also happens when a minister fails. Particularly when that failure involves some kind of sexual misconduct, the fallen colleague becomes fodder for gossip. What good does gossip of this kind do for the kingdom of God? None. We may have to acknowledge in general terms that we know of a minister's resignation, but we need not get into any of the salacious details. We make a great mistake when we assume that a minister who has fallen does not love the Lord. He may love the Lord very much (like King David) and be terribly undisciplined or neurotic when it comes to sexual behavior. His behavior might disqualify him for leadership, but don't assume all of his life and ministry was a sham. It is possible for someone to adore the music of Bach, but play it very badly. Rather than gossip about a man, why not go to him and try to help bind the wounds?

117

What about ministerial behavior to ministers in the ordinary routine of ministry? One of the great offenses is called "sheep stealing." This is the act of deliberately recruiting members from another's congregation. If a minister's work is going well, he may inevitably draw members from another church. One minister said, "I don't steal sheep, but I do plant grass." Certainly, we should never apologize for having a good program. There are, however, acts that do constitute sheep stealing. Some ministers do deliberately target members of other churches by criticizing their church or preacher or trying to make their preacher look bad. Sometimes ministers use the Absalom strategy. Remember how Absalom ingratiated himself with Israel by waiting outside the court? Whenever a person shared with him an unfavorable ruling, he said, "If I were king I would have ruled in your favor." Some ministers employ this strategy and they are anathema. We must remember that they often do it unconsciously, caught up in their own ego needs.

You need to take opportunities to have companionship with other ministers in your circle. There are area, state or city meetings. There are camp and convention committees. While it is possible to overload on these types of activities, to fail to be involved is to rob yourself of a wonderful support system. Some other minister could be a great help to you and you could certainly be of help to another hurting minister.

Sometimes ministers fail to take the opportunity to get to know ministers from other fellowships. Maybe it is seen by some as fraternizing with the enemy. Satan is the enemy, not other ministers. You do not have to give up the doctrines and practices that are precious to you, to have some fellowship with ministers from other circles. In fact, if you really believe in your principles, this might give you an opportunity to share them with a larger audience. No one understands a minister's particular challenges like another minister. You may disagree on doctrine, but find that you agree on philosophy, or at least can give each other sympathy and understanding concerning the problems common to church work. You may have something to learn from these ministers. They may have insight and wisdom that will help you. If nothing else you will learn much about the culture, doctrines and practices of others in the religious world. There are obvious limits to this, but do not limit yourself to contacts made within your own fellowship.

Often you will be asked to give recommendations for a preacher. The request almost always comes from a church that is considering him, not from the preacher himself. Sometimes you can unhesitatingly write a glowing letter of recommendation. Other times are more difficult.

What if he is a competent minister, but you think it would not be a good fit for him to go to this congregation? You write the same letter of recommendation you would in any case, but then you call him on the phone and ask if he really thinks it is the right place for him to serve.

There is also the troubling case of the preacher who is marginally equipped at best and thoroughly incompetent at worst. What do you write? The man needs a job. He has a family to feed. You can write a letter that condemns with faint praise. You need say nothing of his incompetence, but you pick out one area in which you can say something positive. You might write, "As far as I know he is strictly honest: a man who pays his bills and always tells the truth. He is regarded as being a good family man and is respected by his wife and children." Or, you could write, "I can say he has a thorough understanding of Christian doctrine and is committed to it." A wise pulpit committee will notice you did not comment on his pulpit ability, work habits or effectiveness.

What if you are asked to recommend a preacher who has had a moral failure? You have to consider the possibility that he has repented, been forgiven, and regained his character. You cannot write of things that you really don't know though you believe them to be true. You must speak of his competence and you may add that he has made considerable spiritual progress. Then, you may want to suggest they contact a certain person in a certain place. It is a delicate situation. We do not want to rule out forgiven sinners, just as the Lord Jesus did not rule out Peter after he had denied the Lord. On the other hand, we do not want to be party to a situation where offenses are repeated in another place.

Then there is the extreme situation where a minister has actually been arrested. This does occur. What should you do when you are asked to write a letter of recommendation for such a person? You write nothing. You pick up the phone and call the one who wrote you. Suggest over the phone that they may want to talk to the Chief of Police in such and such a town or to some other individual you can name.

Be careful what you put on paper. You must not put in writing accusations you know only from hearsay. The best you can do is refer them to others who have a more exact knowledge of the situation.

Always remember that someday you will need a letter of recommendation from someone. So, when you write such letters be wise and kind. You must always be truthful, but you do not always have to be frank.

CHAPTER EIGHT

THE MINISTER AND THE FUTURE

What will the future hold for the minister? There is no way to be certain. What is certain is that things will change. Change is so rapid that it is said that a computer you buy today is out of date by the time you get it home. Still, it would not hurt us to consider what will face the minister in the 21st century.

One way to look at the changes that lie before us is to think of the changes that lie behind us. The expectations of churches have changed greatly. You are expected to have more expertise in more different fields than ever before. This has led to considerable tension as ministers have often been unable to meet these high and manifold expectations. This trend will likely continue for a while, until it reaches the point of critical mass and churches realize that no one individual can possibly possess so much expertise in so many different fields.

It is certainly foreseeable that daily life for your members will become less and less personal. With data terminals at home, communication over the Internet, and electronic shopping, life will become more and more impersonal. That means that personal contact will be more highly valued than ever before! As the world moves in an impersonal direction ministers and churches will do well to move in the opposite direction. It is a part of human nature to hunger for companionship, approval and fellowship. It will be important that the one place a human being actually answers the phone is the church! It will be important that the one professional in town who knows your name, knows your address, and has actually visited in your home is the minister.

The age of the computer has placed a great temptation before us. It is the temptation to spend all day in front of the screen doing things that seem productive but in fact are not. The computer offers the perfect excuse not to visit, not to meet people in the hospital, home, and workplace. But if you spend all week in front of the computer screen and only appear live in forefront of the congregation on Sunday morning, your sermons will soon lose their relevance and you will soon lose your influence. It is easy to predict that face-to-face contact will be more and more prized and therefore more and more powerful.

One thing about the future is certain. There will be constant change. Tastes in architecture, music, and dress will change. You must be adaptable to change. But when should you change and when should you hold fast? Of course, you will never change your character, your commitment to Christ, your commitment to the church. Methods may need to be changed. How will you know when and what to change? There is good advice in what a Sunday School teacher told a class of teenage girls. They were discussing new fashions and modes of dress. She said, "A Christian young person should not be the first to adopt the new styles — nor the last." Perhaps that's good advice for us ministers. If you are the first to adopt new things they may fail or be very disruptive. If you are the last to change, by that time they will no longer be new but will have been replaced by still other changes. If others have tested the change and found that it works and works well, then you run less risk in attempting that change yourself. So be open to change, but do not be in a hurry to change. Do not change for the sake of change, but change when you see that others have found those changes helpful. And remember that the key is to change enough to attract the new generation without changing so much that you run off the older one.

Yes, the world and the church have always been changing. What makes the work of today's minister even more challenging is the rapidity of that change. Because of our rapid communications, changes happen faster. By the time we get used to one change, it has already been surpassed by a new one. The golden oldies station plays last year's hit songs.

Ministers, as they look toward the future, need to reaffirm some basic tenets. As we reach out to a generation grossly ignorant of the Bible, we have adopted many seeker-sensitive or seeker-driven strategies. Many of the insights from these schools of thought have been quite helpful. But, a looming problem awaits. Eventually the unchurched need to learn the Bible, otherwise what kind of Christians will they be? Unless we are interested in numbers for numbers sake, we cannot adapt everything to the marketers' surveys. In a world that wants to be spiritual without being biblical, ministers need to remain faithful to the Scriptures. If we do not, we may be religious, but we cannot be Christian.

In an age of relativism, ministers need to rededicate themselves to the highest standards. Ministers should not be afraid to be held to a higher standard. While no one should ever be held to an impossible standard, leaders should expect a higher standard. How else could they presume to lead. We need to restore the respect the ministry deserves and needs. It is fashionable today for ministers to complain about their lot. This should never be. No one should pity the minister. He has the greatest opportunity in the world. Some portray the ministry as if it is an impossible job. Not so. It is challenging, but not impossible. When the ministry is going well, there is no greater job in the world. When it is going poorly, there is none worse.

Whatever the challenge, the world needs us more today than ever. No one knows what the future holds. We do not know what new challenges will face those just now entering ministerial education. No one can predict how long the Lord Jesus will tarry. When he comes, may he find us faithfully serving his church. There will always be work for us to do. Jesus said the gates of Hades would not prevail against the church. That means as long as there is life on earth there will be the church. That church can be victorious. That church will need ministers. Fulfill your ministry.

STEWARDSHIP PROMOTION PLAN

It is vital that any stewardship program be the people's program, not just the preacher's program or the program of some individual leader in the congregation. This is accomplished by putting together a large organization. It should not be limited to members of the church board, but should include others with leadership ability who are not members of the board.

The general chairperson should be a person who believes in stewardship and practices it. He or she should be a person who can skillfully handle details and diplomatically oversee the work done by other chairpersons. The general chairperson and the minister will work together as equals and should thoroughly study the program, get it officially approved, and jointly appoint the other leaders.

Committees

The Budget Committee has three tasks. The first is to analyze the giving record of the congregation. Usually the actual work is done by the treasurer or financial secretary, who is already privy to the giving records of the people. Thus there is no eroding of the confidentiality of giving records. The report that is prepared will show only figures (X number of members give X dollars weekly) and percentages (what percent of our members do what percent of the giving).

Their second task is to discover the giving potential. The Chamber of Commerce (Farm Bureau if it is a rural church) can tell you the per capita average annual income. Multiplying this by the number of members and dividing by ten will give you the tithe potential. This should be shown not only in figures but also in terms of projects. (This is what our church could do next year if every member were a tither.) This information must be secured far enough in advance so that ample time can be given to developing a tentative budget.

The third task is budget preparation. Every committee in the church should submit a request for the next year with written justification for any increases and detailed information as to how the money will be spent. Every expenditure should be anticipated (like cleaning the choir robes, buying new hymnals, etc.). When the Budget Committee has completed its budget, it should ask for *tentative* approval from the board. After the campaign is over, the board can again look at the budget and make a final recommendation to the congregation. Every budget is tentative until actually adopted by the congregation. This is not done until after the campaign is over.

Members of the Budget Committee should be carefully selected. A schoolteacher may be better than a banker. You will need people of vision who want to see the church move forward, optimistic people, people who are good givers themselves, and people who are in touch with the actual costs of living and doing business in today's world. (Most retired people tend to think in terms of the economic standards of their productive years and lose touch with the economic realities of the present.)

The Promotion Committee works with the minister and the church secretary in providing and distributing all promotional materials, which might include the following: posters throughout the building (profession-ally done, or from a children's poster contest), hymnbook covers, inserts for the Sunday bulletin, special letters to the congregation, special issues of the church paper, a colorful budget presentation folder (general categories only, no specifics), and tithing testimonies.

Nothing is more effective than tithing testimonies. Ask your treasurer or financial secretary to suggest several names of people who appear to be tithers. Select a representative group (one middle-aged, one young adult, a widow, a retired person, a teen). Ask them to take three minutes at a worship service and tell how God has blessed them through tithing. This should be a very personal talk. It is not to be a biblical argument for tithing. It is to be a personal testimony, a personal experience of God's blessings for the tither. It must be only *three minutes* and should be done at every worship service during stewardship month. The testimonies will be the highlight of the month and will accomplish more than anything else. The minister should work closely with the Promotion Committee in every respect.

The Meals Committee plans the All Church Dinner and also prepares and serves the Canvassers' Breakfast. The All Church Dinner should be catered, preferably outside the church building. It is offered without charge. An offering plate is put at the door for those who want to contribute, but no offering is taken and the dinner is free. This is very important. You want it to be the one dinner of the church year when the women of the church have no work to do.

You'll want the tables to be nicely decorated and the meal tasty and well served. Provide beautiful music, a short but informative presentation of the budget opportunities, and an inspiring talk by a visiting minister or layman.

This committee is also responsible for a Canvassers' Breakfast on the Saturday after Follow-up Sunday. They may ask a Sunday School class to prepare and serve the breakfast, or they may do it themselves.

The Secretarial Committee prepares all mailings, letters, cards, and promotions. A dated chart like the one on pages 139-144 is made up for every committee, and the minister and general chairperson are responsible for seeing that each event occurs on time.

The Telephone Committee phones every member (household) to ask if they plan to come to the All Church Dinner. This needs to be done even though they have already received an invitation in the mail. Only adults and teens attend the dinner. Children are fed at home and then cared for at a separate children's party at the church. The caller reserves a place for the family and determines how many children are coming to the children's party. The number of reservations is reported to the Meals Committee, which then reduces the number by 10% and plans only for 90% of those reserving. (It is better to have to put up an extra table than to have the poor psychological effect of an empty table that was never used.)

The Canvass Committee is a very important committee. Their task is to draft a letter which is sent to every able-bodied male member of the congregation over the age of 21. The letter invites that man to the breakfast and to help collect the pledge cards that are still outstanding. The letter informs them that it is easy work, that it requires them to make no sales talk, and that they will have a partner. The committee phones every person who received the letter asking if he will come and help. This number is then given to the Meals Committee.

The Tally Committee consists of the treasurer and/or financial secretary and other trusted persons who receive the pledge cards on Pledge Sunday, totaling them that afternoon. They do the same on Follow-up Sunday and again on the evening of the Saturday Visitation.

After their totals have been finally recorded, all cards are turned over to the financial secretary for notations to be placed on the giving record sheets for the coming year. Then they are destroyed.

The Prayer Committee arranges a 24-hour chain of prayer just prior to Pledge Sunday. This is a very important part of the total program. Each person is asked to pray for 15 minutes; it takes 96 people to complete the chain. They need not come to the church building, but may pray wherever they are. A chart is placed in the lobby for members to sign. It may be also circulated through adult and youth classes. Finally, it is posted and reminders given in every service and in all publications. The minister and other staff persons should wait and take the hard-to-fill time slots.

Planning a Budget

The giving analysis and tithe potential must be presented to the committee before budget planning begins. Then the budget should be approached on this basis: What is the maximum that we can expect to receive to meet the opportunities before us? Never ask: What is the minimum amount on which the church can be operated? Some even ask all committees to present three budget figures: bare bones minimum, progressive, and ideal. Then these three figures are studied to determine the actual budget figure.

The first set of figures is *missions*. This must never be the last category, but always the first.

The second category is *personnel*. The most important investment a church makes is the investment it makes in people whose talents and skills make the church what it is. After salaries come other personnel expenses: housing, retirement, social security, and amounts for conventions, further education, etc. Auto allowances should NOT come under this category. They are not income to the minister, though they are mistakenly so perceived by some. Auto allowances are an operational expense to the church and that is where they belong.

129

The next category is *worship and education expense.* What will it cost to do a good job with youth, Sunday School, senior citizens, the choirs, the church library, and Vacation Bible School?

Administrative expense is next. What will be the costs for office supplies, postage, equipment, publicity, and stewardship development? Local outreach will include auto allowances, vans, buses, gasoline, radio or TV time, audio cassettes, flowers.

Building and equipment will include utilities, insurance, taxes, and repair and maintenance of property.

The final category is *debt service.*

While the committee wrestles with every little detail of expenditure, the board should receive a little less detail and the congregation only general categories AT THIS TIME. Later, when it is time for the congregation to. in fact adopt the budget, they should receive the same detailed information the board received, but by that time a successful program has raised their sights and given them a realistic view of what the church can do in the coming year.

A colorful folder is printed with pictures. Beside "Maintenance" is a picture of the janitor and a stack of paint cans as high as he is tall. Beside "Personnel" is a picture of the minister shaking hands at the door or standing at the hospital bedside. For every category include a picture that helps people visualize at once what ministry is accomplished, not just what figures are presented.

In the pulpit and newsletter you may present an occasional example from the detailed budget study. Why have we set aside so much for maintenance? Last year a new roof on one of our buildings cost X number of dollars and we anticipate replacing another roof this year. Why is so much set aside for utilities? Our electric bill alone comes to X number of dollars each year.

When you speak of the budget, place the emphasis on the *weekly needs* right up to Pledge Day. The annual figure is printed and mentioned, but it is the weekly figure that should be highlighted. Why? Most people give weekly. We will ask them to pledge weekly. After Pledge Day the annual figure is used. ("Our People Have Pledged XXX Dollars for Next Year.")

After the campaign is over and the board has made a final budget recommendation, then it is presented to the congregation. Many churches do this after the worship service, or possibly during the Sunday School hour if it falls between two services. You might consider instead having it at another dinner (not the one described in this book.) This dinner, too, would include beautiful music and flowers on the tables, but is a carry-in dinner with the church providing the meat, bread and drinks, and the people bringing salad, vegetable or dessert. At that dinner the congregation receives a detailed copy of the budget, modifies it if they wish, and adopts it.

Presenting the Opportunity

People in America have the means to give. Most church people will give if they truly understand the opportunities and needs that face the congregation. The Sunday services present the best forum, but others must also be used. Tithing testimonies are extremely effective. Have a different one at every service if you can (a.m., p.m., Wednesday night). If you cannot do that, you can have at least four, one for each morning worship service during stewardship month.

During the month, one or two sermons on stewardship must come from the pulpit. One should come at the beginning of the month and the other on Pledge Day. Some preachers like to preach on stewardship each Sunday during the month, but most find that is excessive.

In addition to one or two sermons, there could be one Sunday School lesson on stewardship. The regular lesson should be set aside and materials provided for every adult and youth class. Recruit substitutes to teach in case there is a teacher who would be embarrassed to teach this lesson.

The All Church Dinner is an important feature. No offerings are taken and no pledges are made at the dinner. That must be emphasized in all publicity about the dinner.

Any people who pray in public should be reminded privately to pray for the program.

Additional features, described in Section Two, may be useful. Short, dignified pulpit skits may be used, for example, or someone can write a theme chorus or theme song that can be used.

The minister or other creative person must select or adapt a new stewardship theme each year. Some short phrase like "A Bridge to the Future" or "Partners With God" or "Giving Enhances Living" must be chosen. Then put it on posters, bulletin boards, hymnbook covers, church newsletters, and anywhere else you can.

The mail provides another opportunity to communicate the stewardship message. If you do not publish a weekly newsletter, you must do so for this period. If you do, you must make each issue on stewardship a special issue devoted almost exclusively to the program. Change the color of paper or type from the one you always use to a special one for this month. (Avoid red paper or ink — it is hard to read). If you regularly photocopy the paper, have these four issues printed professionally. Use pictures, line drawings, or cartoons. Also, one or more letters should be sent to the entire membership. They may come from the minister and/or the general chairman of the campaign, the chairman of the board, or the chairman of the elders.

The All Church Dinner is an opportunity to share information and to create an atmosphere. After all, the church is a family and should come together as a family. The dinner underscores this biblical concept of the church. Surely the business side of the church is family business. However, children should not attend this dinner. They should be fed at home. A good program provided for them at the church should include games, films, and refreshments. Employ some responsible people from another church to handle this. Every adult and teen member must be free to attend and enjoy the All Church Dinner.

Sometimes sincere people will object to eating a dinner at the church's expense. Remind them that this puts the minister in an awkward position since he eats all his meals at the church's expense, but if they still feel bad about it, they may certainly contribute what their own meal costs. The All Church Dinner is a good investment. No church should be reluctant to spend this money. It will come back a hundredfold.

One of the most effective means of communication is to find an artist who can copy four stewardship cartoons for you. Have them copied onto large poster boards. Put an easel in the lobby and each Sunday in the month put a different one on the easel. Make sure that they are funny. Approaching the subject humorously will disarm the people who get angry at the mention of stewardship. In addition, you may create your own. One might picture a couple walking in front of the church. He has his arm in a sling. She is saying, "It sure looks suspicious on Pledge Day." Another shows a minister speaking to a man who is hiding under a bed. The minister says, "This is our Stewardship Month. I'm so glad I caught you in."

Never divide the budget by the membership thus showing what the average gift would have to be. This is deceptive. Some members give nothing. They never have and they never will. Other members have no means to give. They would like to, but they cannot. But there are other members who can give generously. Resist any effort to publicize each member's share of the budget.

Do show from your records the median gift. That

means half the members gave more and half gave less. Do show and explain the model gift, and the amount given by the largest number of people. Do publicize that X number of members made no gift of record, X number gave less than five dollars weekly, X number gave five to ten, and so forth. Do show that 20% (or 23% or 28%) of the members are doing 80% of the giving.

If people made pledges last year, show the gift of the average pledger and the gift of the average non-pledger. This will demonstrate that few generous givers do not pledge. While there is always a person who is generous and never pledges, most people who say, "I don't believe in pledging," really mean, "I don't believe in giving." If this is your first year for pledging, have the financial secretary indicate on next year's records whether or not the person is a pledger. Then when you repeat the campaign, you can show the dramatic statistics that compare the pledgers and non-pledgers.

Securing Commitments

Prior to Pledge Day the secretary has prepared two pledge cards for every family in the church. The pledge card is just the right size to fit in a windowed envelope. The name and address are pre-printed in just the right place to show through that window. This is the Control File.

On Sunday morning of Pledge Day, after the sermon, hand out blank pledge cards to everyone. Be sure there are pencils in the pews. Read the card and explain it. "The card is not a legal contract. You will receive no bills. It is only a statement of planned giving." Then offer a brief prayer (Only God knows what the future holds; He must guide us here). By all means, if leaders are not comfortable with the word "pledge," call it a giving plan, estimate of giving, or whatever is acceptable. Changing the name of the card is preferable to not having the program at all.

After the prayer ask people to write in the amount they plan to give weekly. The emphasis must be on *weekly*. Then ask them to fill in their name (never ask them to "sign" their name). Then pass the offering plate and ask them to put the cards face down in the plates. Do not do this at the time of the regular offering. It must be special and separate. Ask them to return all cards, both those used and those not used.

That afternoon the Tally Committee should total the number of pledges and calculate the weekly and annual total so it can be announced Sunday night. Then they go to the Control File and pull out both duplicates for every card received with a name on it. Now you have left two cards for each family not pledging. On Monday, send a letter describing in happy tones the results of the previous day. "Already X number of our membership have pledged X number of dollars for next year. Surely when the remaining X number of members respond, we will go over our goal. Many families like theirs were unable to respond Sunday. If they will return the enclosed card by next Sunday, no one will have to visit them. They may return it in the mail or bring it next Sunday." Slip the letter with the preaddressed pledge card into a windowed envelope and mail it. Many will return their card during the week. On Follow-Up Sunday, give people the opportunity to place their cards along with their offering that day.

In the past churches using a program of this type would conclude the program with a personal visit from a member of the church to those who haven't pledged. Even though fund-raising professionals insist it still works, many churches today have deferred to the baby boomer's sensitivity on money expressed by the commonly uttered accusation that a church is only interested in money. If you do not use the home visit, you must have some kind of follow-up. Perhaps you mail a series of letters the next couple of weeks after pledge day to those who did not pledge. The letter would give a positive report on the program and invite the recipient to bring the enclosed card the following Sunday. We cannot stress strongly enough that you must have some kind of follow-up.

If you choose to use the home visit, then the next week the Tally Committee goes again to the Control File and removes the duplicate for all who have responded. When Saturday comes, the men meet for their breakfast. Pair them together and give them the pledge cards with names and addresses already on them. These are their assignments. Try to group them geographically.

Instruct these men that they are not to try to persuade anyone. Anyone not now persuaded is not going to be. They are merely to say, "We came to pick up the card you received in the mail." If the person says it is lost, the caller says, "We have the duplicate here that you may use." When the work is finished, all cards are to be returned to the Tally Committee.

Remind these people that their function is not to raise money. Some people deliberately held out their cards because they were lonely. They wanted a visit. Some really forgot or were out of town. Some will want an opportunity to air some grievance. They should listen politely, but neither agree nor disagree. Sometimes people need to vent their feelings. Then they get over them. The callers must keep completely confidential everything that happens. They may tell the minister only if it is something he needs to know. Otherwise, they are to tell no one anything that transpired on their visits.

Now, a question: Why was every man invited to participate? There are two reasons. The first is that it turns up unexpected talent. The second is that it disarms the person who is visited. He knows how that man got that job. It was a job he refused to do. That prepares him to treat the visit kindly and courteously.

Another question: Why were women not included in

this canvass calling? The reason is merely a practical one. By restricting the callers to one gender you avoid the problem of sending out a man with another man's wife or vice versa. This visitation program is simply easier to organize if the callers are all men.

The follow-up program will not bring in many pledges, but it is absolutely essential. If people did not know that some kind of follow-up was part of the program, many would procrastinate and not pledge. But because they know that it is part of the program, they go ahead and cooperate in the earlier stages. You simply must not omit this part of the plan.

Nor should you go through the cards and select some not to be contacted. You have no right to decide who will or will not make a pledge. This is their decision.

Completing the Program

A letter is sent to all pledgers thanking them for their pledge, but without mentioning the amount.

Offering envelopes are prepared for every family in the church. They are placed on tables alphabetically arranged for people to pick them up at church. All not picked up are mailed.

Quarterly receipts are mailed to every giver. You can purchase from your Christian bookstore any one of several systems that will assist in keeping track of these gifts and making these reports. Try to find a system that makes multiple copies with one entry. Using this, the financial secretary need record a gift only once. They have four copies to be mailed one each quarter, and a final copy to be kept in the files.

Mailing these quarterly receipts is absolutely necessary. Emphasize that they are receipts, not bills. If there are mistakes they should be detected before an IRS audit, not afterward. The quarterly mailing of receipts keeps everyone up to date.

The church board abides by the budget, but recognizes the right to make changes as the year goes along. However, those changes should not amount to more than 10% of the gross budget.

Each quarter the Finance Committee should review the receipts, expenditures and the budget, and if necessary, present a revised budget.

Stewardship Calendar

Prior to Stewardship Month

COMMITTEE	TASK	COMPLETION DATE	
BUDGET	Complete giving analysis; study giving potential; prepare tentative budget	Monday	
SECRETARIAL	Begin assembly of family unit file	Monday	
BOARD	Approve budget goals	Tuesday	
MINISTER	Order materials	Thursday	
MINISTER	Place printing orders	Friday	
ALL	Full organization meets for briefing	Sunday	
PROMOTION	Begin securing tithing testimonies and teacher commitments	Sunday	

*When each task has been completed, put a checkmark in the right hand column

First Week of Campaign

COMMITTEE	TASK	COMPLETION DATE	
OFFICE	Begin print work	Monday	
SECRETARIAL	Mail church paper #1	Wednesday	
SECRETARIAL	All print work completed	Friday	
SECRETARIAL	Mail dinner invitations	Friday	
PROMOTION	Complete securing of tithing testimonies and teacher commitments; first tithing testimony	Sunday	
SECRETARIAL	Bulletin inserts	Sunday	
MINISTER	Campaign announcements	Sunday	

Second Week of Campaign

COMMITTEE	TASK	COMPLETION DATE	
SECRETARIAL	Letter to all male members	Monday	
SECRETARIAL	Mail church paper #2	Wednesday	
CANVASS	Meeting of Canvass Team Captains; begin securing canvassers	Wednesday	
PRAYER	Begin prayer enlistment	Wednesday	
SECRETARIAL	Complete family file	Friday	
TELEPHONE	Phone all re: Dinner	Saturday	
SECRETARIAL	Bulletin inserts	Sunday	
PROMOTION	Second tithing testimony	Sunday	
PROMOTION	Stewardship lesson in Bible school	Sunday	

Third Week of Campaign

COMMITTEE	TASK	COMPLETION DATE	
SECRETARIAL	Mail church paper #3	Wednesday	
ALL	All Church Dinner	Wednesday	
PROMOTION	Third tithing testimony	Sunday	
SECRETARIAL	Bulletin inserts	Sunday	
MINISTER	Campaign announcements	Sunday	

Fourth Week of Campaign

COMMITTEE	TASK	COMPLETION DATE	
SECRETARIAL	Mail church paper #4	Wednesday	
CANVASS CAPTAINS	Complete recruiting of canvassers	Wednesday	
PRAYER	Complete prayer enlistment	Wednesday	
MEALS	Complete plans for canvassers' breakfast	Wednesday	
ALL	11:00 a.m. begin 24-hour chain of prayer	Saturday	
ALL	Pledge Day	Sunday	
MINISTER	Stewardship sermon	Sunday	
PROMOTION	Fourth tithing testimony	Sunday	
PROMOTION	Church Night — P.M.	Sunday	

Follow-up Week #1

COMMITTEE	TASK	COMPLETION DATE	
SECRETARIAL	Mail letters and pledge cards to all not pledging Sunday	Monday	
TELEPHONE	Instruct telephone committee	Monday	
ALL	Follow-up Sunday	Sunday	

Follow-up Week #2

TELEPHONE	Phone all canvassers	Monday	
SECRETARIAL	Mail letters to all canvassers	Thursday	
CANVASSERS	Assignment for all canvassers	Saturday	
TALLY & MEALS	Breakfast	Saturday	

APPENDIX B

TALENT SURVEY FORM

Anywhere Christian Church
MINISTRY INTEREST SURVEY
Keeping Matthew 25:14-30 in mind, please fill this out carefully and return it as soon as possible.

NAME _____ ADDRESS _____

OCCUPATION _____ PHONE _____

Circle the activities in which you have experience.
X the activities in which you have an interest.
Make any comments you feel would be helpful.

PERSONAL WORK
1__ Usher
2__ Visit the sick
3__ Church calling
4__ Counseling
5__ Greeter
6__ Planning socials
7__ Befriend new people
8__ Provide transportation
   (chauffeur's license?)
9__ Child care (baby-sit,
   nursery help)
10__ Children's teacher/ leader/ helper
11__ Home nursing
12__ Chaperone youth groups
13__ Entertain guests
14__Other_____

PUBLIC TEACHING
1__ Lead devotions
2__ Sunday school teacher
   What age?_____
3__ Choir leader
   What age?_____
4__ VBS teacher/ helper
5__ What kind of group would you like
   to lead?

SKILLED SERVICE
1__ Building upkeep
2__ Yard work
3__ Hauling/driving
4__ Floral arrangements
5__ Photography
6__ Keep records
7__ Repair equipment
8__ Sewing
9__ Carpentry
10__ Other _____

OFFICE/ ADMINISTRATIVE
1__ Office work
2__ Typing
   computer?_____
3__ Printing
4__ Prepare news articles
5__ Keep records
6__ Filing
7__ Librarian
8__ Publicity
9__ Graphic design
10__ Other_____

CREATIVE ARTS
1__ Singing in a group
2__ Singing a solo
3__ Play an instrument
   Which?_____
4__ Worship leading
   Age group_____
5__ Choir/ensemble director
   Age group_____
6__ Special program help
   In what way?_____
7__ Acting
8__ Directing
9__ Script writing
10__ Stage/props managing
11__ Set design/ construction
12__ Sound technician
13__ Lighting technician
14__ Multimedia/slides
15__ Worship planning
16__ Worship team
17__ Art work
18__ Creative writing
19__ Newsletter layout
20__ Bulletin layout/printing

Do you have a hobby? ____ If so, what? _____
THANK YOU FOR YOUR HELP!

147

CHECKLIST FOR AN EFFECTIVE WEDDING

_____ Set a tentative date and decide on the type of wedding

_____ Decide on the time and place

_____ Make arrangements with the minister and/or church

_____ Reserve the church or site of wedding

_____ Reserve a reception location

_____ Make arrangements with caterers

_____ Select attendants

_____ Select florist

_____ Select photographer

_____ Select soloist and instrumentalists

_____ Plan rehearsal dinner

_____ Compile list of friends and relatives to be invited

_____ Order wedding invitations

_____ Decide on clothes

_____ List silver, china, and crystal patterns

_____ Decide on reception hostess

_____ Mail invitations

_____ Bride and groom purchase gifts

_____ Purchase rings

_____ Purchase guest book

_____ Decide on music selections
_____ Plan honeymoon
_____ Make housing arrangements for guests
_____ Send announcement to newspaper
_____ Apply for license
_____ Confirm details with florist
_____ Try on clothes
_____ Pack for the honeymoon
_____ Attend rehearsal
_____ Take care of honoraria to minister, soloist and accompanist
_____ Get to the church early
_____ Have the ceremony
_____ Attend the reception
_____ Leave for honeymoon

JOB HUNTING

Job hunting can be a terribly frustrating experience. For years we have recruited ministers by talking about a preacher shortage — if there really is such a thing. Most churches report having anywhere from 30-60 resumes for their openings. The hardest job to get is your first job. More than academic credentials, a pulpit committee wants to see your track record. What makes this process particularly frustrating is that churches take a long time in determining the call and are often not forthcoming with information as to the status of the search. It is not unusual for churches to take six months or more to make a decision. Sometimes they will make a decision and fail to inform you.

Pulpit committees are notoriously quirky, so any attempt to give advice on how to apply for a position is fraught with dangers. Every committee takes on its own unique personality with its own unique agendas. If you are to make it through this process with your self-esteem intact, you must understand that your talent and ability is often a small part of the decision. With that disclaimer we can discuss a typical process.

Where do you find information about open pulpits?

In a church tradition without bishops or regional denominational headquarters, you have a well-developed grapevine. Bible colleges and seminaries usually keep a master list of churches who have reported openings to them. You can also look in the appropriate church magazines. Perhaps the best source of information is other ministers. You can let your need be known to a prominent minister in the community, and he may be in a position to give you information or to recommend you. Sometimes the church comes to you. That is flattering, but even then you can't count on getting the job.

When you start the process of interviewing, you will typically be asked for a resume. Make sure the resume is flawless. Its purpose is to sell you as a competent minister. It should include, by category, personal data, education, work experience, publications, community activities, and awards and honors. Frequently you will be asked to submit an audio or video cassette of one of your sermons. It is good to put a personal face on the decision, so try to meet someone from the committee if possible. Some churches will give a preliminary interview by phone. Others may choose to have you write out some questions and answers. Be careful your answers to these questions don't get you embroiled in the middle of some church squabble.

Evenutally you will be asked for some kind of personal interview. Be on time. Be friendly. Look your best. To give yourself confidence, try to anticipate some of the questions you think they will ask and frame some answers. It is all right for you to ask them questions. It is a poor interview if you don't. Some committees are hoping to learn something about you from the way you ask questions, not just answer them.

If the committee decides on you, then there is a trial sermon. How do you get away to do that? You can work it around a vacation or your allotted speaking engagements. Sometimes they may ask you to come and speak for a banquet or the like. Rarely should you go for a trial sermon until you are virtually certain you will get the call and virtually certain that you will accept it. Once your present congregation finds out you are hunting for a new church, you will be the proverbial lame duck. When you schedule a trial sermon, you should arrange for a guest speaker to fill in. On the day before you leave, tell the chairman of the elders or chairman of the board (whoever is considered the highest ranking member of the congregational leadership) that you will be out of the pulpit and you have arranged for a fill-in preacher.

The congregation will vote on you after the service or the following Sunday. What kind of vote should you expect? A unanimous vote is rare, particularly on a secret ballot. You are probably safe to accept a call at 80% or above.

Once you have accepted the new position, you should read your letter of resignation at the close of the service. If you do this at the beginning, it will cast a pall over the whole morning worship experience. The days after you have announced your resignation will be the most difficult days of your ministry. The people who are closest to you will treat you the worst; this is mostly because they feel rejected. The sooner you can exit the better. If the church is willing to pay you for the thirty or sixty days and let you get on with the transition, you should probably accept. Nevertheless, some good can be done during the transition. Some people who have been putting off a decision will choose to act so that you might be able to be involved. You will get extremely tired of saying good-bye every day for a month or two. Always go out with a gracious spirit. Even if you have had a difficult relationship with the church, it is not the time to get even. It might make you feel good, but it will not do any good.

One solemn word of warning to you. Never resign from a church until you have the next church signed, sealed and delivered. You might think other churches will be clamoring for your services, but you might be surprised. You have a family to care for. You also don't want the reputation of being a quitter. It is easier to get a job when you have a job. No matter how mad or upset you are, don't resign until you have another church.

BIBLIOGRAPHY

Administration

Brown, Lowell. *Sunday School Standards: A Guide for Measuring & Achieving Sunday School Success.* Ventura, CA: Regal Books, 1981.

Criswell, W.A. *Criswell's Guidebook For Pastors.* Nashville: Broadman, 1980.

Engstrom, Ted and Edward Dayton. *The Christian Executive.* Waco: Word Books, 1979.

_____. *The Art of Management for Christian Leaders.* Waco: Word Books, 1979.

_____. *Strategy for Living.* Ventura: Regal Books, 1982.

George, Carl. *Leading and Managing Your Church.* Old Tappan, NJ: Revell, 1990.

Hyles, Jack. *The Hyles Church Manual.* Murfreesboro, TN: Sword of the Lord, 1968.

Leas, Speed. *Time Management: A Working Guide for Church Leaders.* Nashville: Abingdon, 1980.

Powers, Bruce. *Church Administration Handbook.* Nashville: Broadman, 1985.

Stone, Sam. *The Christian Minister*. Cincinnati: Standard, 1991.

Towns, Elmer. *The Successful Sunday School and Teachers Guidebook*. Carol Stream, IL: Creation House, 1976.

Wemp, C. Sumner. *A Guide to Practical Pastoring*. New York: Thomas Nelson, 1982.

Williman, Anne and Steven Clark. *Pastor's Complete Model Letter Book*. New York: Prentice-Hall, 1989.

Church Growth

Aldrich, Joseph. *Life-Style Evangelism*. Portland: Multnomah Press, 1981.

Arn, Charles and Donald Mc Gavran. *Growth: A New Vision for the Sunday School.* Pasadena: Church Growth Press, 1980.

Arn, Win and Charles Arn. *The Master's Plan for Making Disciples*. Monrovia: Church Growth, 1982.

Barna, George. *User Friendly Churches: What Christians Need to Know About the Churches People Love to Go to*. Ventura, CA: Regal Books, 1991.

——————. *The Frog in the Kettle: What Christians Need to Know about Life in the Year 2,000*. Ventura, CA: Regal Books, 1990.

Bisagno, John. *How to Build an Evangelistic Church*. Nashville: Broadman, 1971.

Callahan, Kennon. *Twelve Keys to an Effective Church*. San Francisco: Harper & Row, 1983.

Dudley, Carl. *Making the Small Church Effective*. Nashville: Abingdon, 1978.

Ellis, Joe. *The Church on Purpose*. Cincinnati: Standard, 1985.

MacGavran, Donald and Win Arn. *How to Grow a Church: Conversations about Church Growth*. Glendale, CA: Regal Publishers, 1975.

——————. *Ten Steps for Church Growth*. Nashville: Discipleship Resources, 1982.

MacGavran, Donald and George Hunter. *Church Growth: Strategies That Work*. Nashville: Abingdon, 1981.

Miller, Herb. *The Vital Congregation*. Nashville: Abingdon, 1990.

Moorehead, Bob. *The Growth Factor*. Joplin: College Press, 1988.

Schaller, Lyle. *44 Ways to Increase Church Attendance*. Nashville: Abingdon, 1988.

—————. *44 Questions for Church Planters*. Nashville: Abingdon, 1991.

—————. *Activating the Passive Church: Diagnosis and Treatment*. Nashville: Abingdon, 1983.

—————. *Growing Plans: Strategies to Increase Your Church's Membership*. Nashville: Abingdon, 1983.

—————. *Middle Sized Church: Problems and Prescriptions*. Nashville: Abingdon, 1985.

Towns, Elmer. *The Complete Book of Church Growth*. Wheaton: Tyndale House, 1981.

Vaughan. John. *The World's 20 Largest Churches*. Grand Rapids: Baker, 1984.

Wagner, Peter. *Leading Your Church to Growth*. Ventura, CA: Regal Books, 1984.

—————. *Your Church Can Grow*. Ventura, CA: Regal Books, 1982.

Counseling

Adams, Jay E. *The Christian Counselor's Manual*. Grand Rapids: Baker, 1973.

—————. *Coping With Counseling Crises*. Grand Rapids: Baker,1978.

—————. *Competent To Counsel*. Grand Rapids: Baker, 1970.

Anderson, Ray. *Christians Who Counsel*. Grand Rapids: Zondervan, 1990.

Collins, Gary. *Christian Counseling: A Comprehensive Guide*. Waco: Word Books, 1980.

Crabb, Lawrence. *Effective Biblical Counseling*. Grand Rapids: Zondervan, 1977.

Hamilton, James. *The Ministry of Pastoral Counseling*. Grand Rapids: Baker, 1972.

Kirwan, William. *Biblical Concepts for Christian Counseling*. Grand Rapids: Baker, 1984.

McKenna, David. *The Psychology of Jesus: The Dynamics of Christian Wholeness*. Waco: Word Books, 1977.

Minirth, Frank. *Christian Psychiatry*. New York: Revell, 1977.

Oates, Wayne. *An Introduction to Christian Counseling*. Nashville: Broadman, 1959.

_____. *Behind the Masks*. Philadelphia: Westminster, 1987.

Stone, Howard. *Crisis Counseling*. Philadelphia: Fortress, 1986.

Wright, Norman. *Crisis Counseling: Helping People in Crisis and Stress*. San Bernardino: Here's Life Publications, 1985.

_____. *Training Christians to Counsel*. Eugene: Harvest House Publishing, 1977.

Conflict Management

Burton, John. *Conflict Resolution and Prevention*. New York: St. Martin's Press, 1990.

Dale, Robert. *Surviving Difficult Church Members*. Nashville: Abingdon, 1984.

Deutsch, M. *The Resolution of Conflict: Constructive and Destructive Process*. New Haven: Yale University Press, 1973.

Fenton, Horace. *When Christians Clash*. Downers Grove: InterVarsity Press, 1987.

Flynn, Leslie. *When the Saints Come Storming In*. Wheaton: Victor Books, 1988.

Lowry, Randolph. *Crisis Management and Counseling*. Waco: Word Books, 1991.

McSwain, Larry and William Treadwell. *Conflict Ministry in the Church*. Nashville: Broadman, 1981.

Sande, Ken. *The Peacemaker: A Biblical Guide to Resolving Personal Conflict*. Grand Rapids: Baker, 1991.

Weddings and Funerals

Peterson, Eugene and Calvin Miller. *Weddings, Funerals, and Special Events*. Waco: Word Books, 1987.

Wallis, Charles. *The Funeral Encyclopedia: A Source Book*. New York: Harper & Row, n.d.